Apartment Gardening

Mediterranean Style

TERRACES, BALCONIES AND WINDOWSILLS

Clodagh & Dick Handscombe

Apartment Gardening Mediterranean Style

Published by Ediciones Santana, S.L.
Apartado 41
29650 Mijas-Pueblo (Málaga)
Spain

Tel: (0034) 952 48 58 38
E-Mail: info@santanabooks.com
Website: www.santanabooks.com

Copyright © 2010 Clodagh and Dick Handscombe

Photography and illustrations:
Generally by the authors with credit given for specific photographs to Alsol, Eric Furio,
Georgi Helnz of Floraguard, Graf Ibérica, Harrod Horticulture, Ian Baker, Julia Evans of Arthouse,
Lynne Godfrey of Jigsaw Design, Jordi Domingo Calabuig, Margaret McRobert, Maurizio Makovec of
Onopiu, Miguel Angel Gómez, Paco Callado, Peter Gudgeon, Soljardi, The Organic Catalogue, The
Roof Garden (Kensington, London), Tom Horner and Toni Ramírez.

Designed by Cheryl Gatward of newimage.es

No part of this book may be reproduced or transmitted in any form or by any means without the prior
written permission of the publishers.

Printed in Spain by Gráficas San Pancracio, S.L.

ISBN: 978-84-89954-86-1
Depósito Legal: MA-755/2010

Where electronic addresses of useful organisations are mentioned they were correct at the time of
going to press. Their inclusion by the authors does not imply that the authors or publishers endorse
their services or products. Likewise, where practical solutions to problems are given there is no
guarantee by the publishers or authors that they will be appropriate or work in every situation.

Dedication

To the millions of people living in apartments in Spain and other Mediterranean climate situations and to our parents who stimulated our early interest in gardening in containers.

Acknowledgements

This book would not have been born without the motivation of seeing the many apartment terraces, balconies and windowsills in Spain and other Mediterranean-climate countries just waiting for improvement.

We thank our publishers Gertrud and Alan Roberts for commissioning the book, our good friend Patricia Philson for reviewing a draft, son Robin Lee for solving computer problems at a critical stage, and our designer Cheryl Gatward and Gráficas San Pancracio, the printers, for turning our vision into a splendid reality.

Contents

4 Successful Terrace, Balcony and Windowsill Plants

5 Caring for your Plants

6 Types of Containers to Use

7 Growing Culinary and Medicinal Herbs

8 Container-grown Fruit

9 Container-grown Vegetables

10 Dealing with Pests and Diseases

11 Seasonal Apartment Gardening Calendars

Introduction

Apartment Gardening Mediterranean Style is the complete guide to gardening on terraces, balconies and windowsills in small and large apartments located on the Mediterranean coast or inland. It is designed to help full and part-time residents make them more colourful, productive and liveable. The scope for improvements is enormous.

There are millions of people living in apartments in Spain and other Mediterranean climate locations worldwide. Yet when one looks at apartment buildings only some 10 to 15 per cent of terraces balconies and windowsills show signs of plants in pots and window boxes or of being regularly used as attractive and productive outdoor living spaces. The best incorporate to varying degrees facilities for enjoying the sun and alfresco eating and drinking with the growing of flowering and evergreen plants, herbs, fruit and vegetables. All of which can be easily grown with the help of modern-day containers and composts provided plants sensible for the microclimate of your location are selected. In some respects growing things for an apartment owner is easier and less time-consuming than for the owner of a villa surrounded by a sizeable plot of poor soil.

Apartment Gardening Mediterranean Style presents practical ideas, guidelines and solutions to the problems related to merely adding a few containers of flowering plants and a lemon tree or to designing, developing and maintaining a fully-fledged terrace garden and living space – a personal-style Garden of Eden or Shangri-La in the skies. The book is intensively illustrated to provide insights into good and not-so-good practices and to stimulate your creativity and originality. For, in practice, no two people have the same vision of how they want to spend their time on the Med; the role their apartment terraces, balconies and smaller windowsills could play in making the best of that time; and the style of plants and containers they would like to have.

Both experienced and novice gardeners will find the book of interest. For the latter we include basic gardening good practices and skills.

We hope that you will enjoy using the book as a comprehensive handbook to guide and support you in the coming months and years as have the sister books *Your Garden in Spain, Growing Healthy Fruit in Spain* and *Growing Healthy Vegetables in Spain,* written primarily for owners of houses.

Clodagh and Dick
Spain 2010

Your opportunities and challenges

There are good reasons why everyone with an apartment or flat in Spain or other Mediterranean climate areas should make full use of their valuable terrace, balcony and windowsill spaces to establish a comfortable, visually appealing and productive outside living space which looks attractive to neighbours and passers-by. Achieving this is within everyone's ability.

1.1 Your Personal Opportunities

Congratulations! You have purchased or rented an apartment or penthouse comprising an enclosed living area and open balconies, terraces and windowsills. Large or small these represent a high percentage of the total floor area of your investment so put them to good use. Achieve the full benefit of having covered or open space in the generally wonderful Mediterranean climate in which you have chosen to live. A climate for living outdoors for much of the year and in which a multitude of plants can be grown in small spaces. Not only flowers but also ecological fruit herbs and vegetables.

However small ,large or high up your apartment you have four fundamental opportunities:

* Create an appealing and comfortable outdoor room.
* Make the best use of the limited space you have.
* Grow at least some of the time herbs, fruit and vegetables.
* Improve the appearance of the apartment block and neighbourhood in which you live.

And what's more compared to gardening in a garden surrounding a house:

* You can garden day and night by the lights of the terrace.
* On a covered terrace you can still work when it rains and not get muddy feet.
* By pulling the blind down you can work when it's cold.
* Many things can be done standing up or sitting down on a stool without straining one's back.
* You can change the position of plant containers and indeed change the total layout several times a year.

This book is here to help you improve what you have already done or start from scratch. Whether you wish to create a mini Garden of Eden or Shangri-la, hang a couple of window boxes on the railings or perhaps just add a perpetual fruiting Lemon tree, there is something for all. Much can be done in a short time whether retired, working or a student.

But your start point will depend on the type of apartment you have and it's present state.

1.2 What Type of Apartment do you Have?

The number and sizes of outdoor spaces that you will have depends on the architectural design of the building which houses the apartment. We illustrate on the opposite page five types of apartment buildings that exist along the Costas and inland today. They will be easily recognised and the sequence of five buildings follows the evolution of styles in Spain and other Mediterranean climate situations.

They can be described as follows:

I is a typical two-storey village or town house with an added floor converted into three apartments.

II is a building in which individual apartments run from the front to back.

III differs in that there are separate front and back apartments and pent houses.

IV illustrates a pyramid block with back-to-back apartments on each floor.

V represents a Benidorm high-rise, apartment block with a penthouse.

On each building we indicate the typical location of windowsills, balconies, terraces, closed open and glazed.

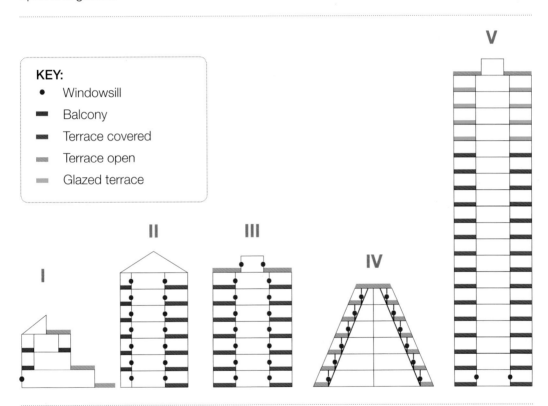

KEY:
- • Windowsill
- ▬ Balcony
- ▬ Terrace covered
- ▬ Terrace open
- ▬ Glazed terrace

Our estimate is that no more than 10 to 15 per cent of those windowsills, balconies and terraces are well-used. Just look around. A glance from a balcony, over terrace railings or through a window and a short stroll around many neighbourhoods will immediately illustrate the scale of the current opportunities. Rarely does one find an entire apartment block – whether three or 30 stories high – which looks lived in and cared for. Just occasionally one sees a block with every balcony and terrace railings bedecked with colourful and evergreen pots and window boxes creating a Hanging Gardens of Babylon effect.

What one sees can be described in a number of ways. The most relevant are as follows:

Terraces

A planted up patio or small garden in the sky, a covered or open extra room, the most used room of the apartment, or a wasted space, an outdoor utility room, a store room or an eye-sore.

Balconies

A flower bed in the sky, an outdoor greenhouse, a greening of the neighbourhood , an urban allotment. Or a convenient storage area, an eye-sore of pots and/or window boxes filled with dead plants, with nothing to make it an appealing area to live in.

Windowsills

A micro balcony, an attractive bouquet or plant collection, or a bottle bank, a nothing, an untidy forgotten plant graveyard or a mess.

What do you have today? What change would you like to make? You won't be alone in having the opportunity to make better use of your open or covered terrace, balcony and windowsill spaces. Today there are around eight billion persons in the world and probably more than half live in apartments with terraces of various sizes and shapes. What an opportunity for improving not just your neighbourhood but the world in which we live.

Photographs of a wide variety of windowsills, balconies and terraces of all sizes and styles will be discussed in Parts Two and Three.

▲ A neglected block   ▲ A looked after block

1.3 Typical Sizes of Terraces Balconies and Windowsills

Naturally what you can achieve will depend on the space you have.

Terraces, balconies and windowsills come in a range of sizes: typically windowsills from a fifth to a full square metre, balconies from one to 10 square metres and terraces ranging from only two to 200 or more square metres. The largest penthouse terrace can accommodate a fully landscaped garden and a typical balcony may only have space for a line of window boxes or pots. While the former offers reasonable living space, the latter may allow you to do more than stand outside to admire the view or to stretch your legs when sitting in the blacony doorway.

In practice terrace space alone can range from 10 to 50 per cent of the size of the internal accommodation, as illustrated in the table below.

Type of Property	Total area m²	Total terrace m²	% Terrace space of property
Studio apartment	50	10 – 20	20 – 40
One bedroom apartment	70	7 – 14	10 – 20
Three bedroom apartment	100	15 – 20	15 – 20
Small penthouse	200	50 – 100	25 – 50

So, if at present your terrace/s are totally undeveloped, it is a significant under-utilisation of the property you have purchased or inherited.

1.4 Making Best Use of the Space You Have

However small or large your terraces, balconies and windowsills there are a number of generic things that can be done on them to make them more appealing, more frequently used and more productive (see table below.) These possibilities are enlarged on in Part Two for windowsills and balconies and in Part Three for terraces.

What can be done?	To windowsills?	To balconies?	To terraces?
Brighten them up with flowering and evergreen plants in pots and window boxes etc..	Yes	Yes	Yes
Add leisure and or sun chairs	No	*Yes	Yes
Transform into an outside covered room	No	No	*Yes
Transform into open air patio style room	No	No	*Yes
Establish a collection of herbs	**Yes	Yes	Yes
Grow a few fruits perhaps starting with a perpetual lemon tree or grape vine.	***Yes	**Yes	Yes
Grow a few vegetables	**Yes	Yes	Yes

Note: *Only if furniture is small in size. ** Extent dependent on size. *** Just strawberries.

1.5 What an Opportunity for a Creative Hobby!

The table on the previous page illustrates the scope for creativity and how interesting terrace, balcony and windowsill gardening can be as a hobby. It can be just as fascinating and rewarding as designing developing and maintaining a full-sized garden around a villa.

Most people have more creative talents than they think. You don't need to be a qualified architect, interior decorator, gardener or artist to make effective changes to your apartment. Just look around you and see the variations in the style of apartment blocks built in the recent years. In many cases it requires amateur owner-gardeners to transform unattractive architecture into an attractive place to live by transforming terraces and balconies. Look at the wonderful gardens developed by dedicated amateur gardeners around their villas. The opportunities for apartment dwellers are just as great.

But don't just look around and copy the designs of the pioneers but think out something unique that matches what you – and when relevant the family – want from Spain or another Mediterranean climate situation. Learn to garden in containers. There is much to be done on a small scale. For instance just one square metre can fit in 36 15cm pots, 12 50cm window boxes, three large troughs and one raised bed or growing table.

You are not going to be able to import 5,000 square metres of one-and-a-half metres of topsoil as was done in London in the 1930s to create the roof-top Spanish Garden six floors up in Kensington with 75 full-sized trees, Alhambra-style fountains, a stream with shoals of fish etc. but you can achieve something more intimate and liveable in.

If you attempt a total redevelopment of a terrace you will soon be using your perhaps previously hidden skills as an interior designer, artist and gardener or you will soon develop them. Failing that you can always find somebody to do the work for you once you have decided what it is you want. Even window boxes can be planted up by the best garden centres for a small fee.

1.6 Adding Value to Property and Location

At the time of writing there are more than a million apartments for sale just along the Mediterranean coast with Spain having the most. And there also hundreds of thousands inland. If you are thinking of selling, improve the appearance and usability of your terraces, balconies and window ledges to create a more attractive saleable property with unique features but minimum maintenance. In recent years rooftop allotments on top of new apartment blocks in London have been sold for 150,000 euros. A collection of vegetables and fruit trees growing in containers may be the key to selling an expensive penthouse or small studio.

▲ Spanish Garden, Kensington. Something more achieveable ▶

1.7 Contributing to the Local Environment

Many individual apartments, entire blocks and communities look deserted, unused and uncared for on the coast and in the cities – even though many are lived in for all or most of the year by the owners, holiday-making tenants or student groups. It's a great shame and indeed an environmental disaster for both nature and people. Only two, three or four decades ago – depending on the region – today's totally urbanised, concrete jungle found along the Mediterranean was virgin coastline, with small fishing villages or agricultural areas growing fruit and vegetables. If one drove along the motorway above Benidorm, acres of tomatoes grew on either side, and north of Estepona in Málaga vegetables were grown between the main road and the beach as in many lengths of the coast line. Now, except in public parks, strips alongside developments, gardens in the better class of community and around villas, often not a flowering plant is to be seen on more than 10 to 15 per cent of apartment terraces, balconies and windowsills. Town centres and northern towns and villages tend to fare better. In fact northern and inland blocks of flats – mostly inhabited by Spaniards – are more noticeable for their summer floral colour and daily use of terraces and balconies.

Increasingly there is a growing network of people tending terrace vegetable gardens or urban huertas (allotments) as they have been termed. Even a single window box and a container of home-grown vegetables – especially if grown ecologically – could start to make a difference to the area in which you live. We note that the world's most gardened nation – Britain – with probably the highest percentage of people growing at least some of their own vegetables – launched a 2010 national campaign called 'One pot pledge' coordinated by the Garden Organic charity.

What we need in Spain is the British and French system of 'Best village and town awards' in all regions and a 'Pledge a window box' campaign. Imagine the impact if every apartment block had a 'Window Box Circle' with some members designing seasonal window box displays and others potting them up.

1.8 Reduce your Carbon Footprint

One does not have to be an ecologist to recognise that changing much of the Mediterranean coastline from a naturally green landscape to the concrete landscape of recent decades has resulted in climate changes. A climate of a warmer summer sea, fewer summer storms and more autumn rains and perhaps a return to colder winters. Many claim that the main cause is the massive increase in carbon dioxide emissions and the lack of plant life to absorb this gas to produce plant nutrients and the chlorophyll that greens each and every plant. More and more we are deluged with propaganda to reduce our household carbon footprints.

Doing so by:

- Using fewer plastic bags and containers and recycling paper cardboard tins bottles etc. that all use CO2-producing fossil fuels in their manufacture
- Using sun and wind-power electricity, solar al fresco cooking equipment
- Maximising the benefit of low winter suns warming south-facing apartments.
- Most importantly, even on an apartment terrace planting plants that absorb carbon dioxide and convert it into plant nutrients and chlorophyll – the greening agent for plants.

Having seen the 5000-square-metre rooftop Spanish Garden in London closely planted with full-size trees and shorter plants and a 1000-square-metre rooftop cacti garden in Gran Canarias, we can dream of the impact it would make if each and every apartment and office block was required to have a roof garden for the benefit of residents and employees or just to digest CO_2 and re-green the Costas when seen from the air.

That's very unlikely, but if every apartment terrace window box and windowsill was 'green' it would make a local contribution.

1.9 Contribution to Your Well-being

One thing that is often highlighted in publicity material – but sometimes missed or soon forgotten – is that the Mediterranean climate areas of the world are among the best zones of the world for the healthy living of plants, animals and humans. It therefore makes good sense to maximise the possibilities for using your covered and open terraces to:

- Use the free sun to build up your vitamin D intake on as many days as possible – spring summer, autumn and winter – by careful sunbathing.
- Live the rest of the day in a stimulating as well as relaxing environment.
- Grow aromatic, perfumed flowers but also healthy ecological herbs, fruit and vegetables that can be harvested fresh when at their best.
- Eat well with your own healthily grown foods full of natural vitamins and minerals without

the risks of chemical contamination and at the same time save cash as you will not have to purchase so much food and will spend less on travel costs. On 10th December 2009 the International Slow food organisation held 1000 simultaneous gastronomic events to highlight the need for more communities to strive for an increase in the local production of quality foodstuffs with a fair return to the grower. What better place to start than on your terrace if you don't have a garden or allotment? As the photograph shows, much can be done in only one square metre of space.

Parts Seven Eight and Nine discuss in turn the mini-growing of herbs, fruits and vegetables respectively.

1.10 Terraces Make Friends

Once you start to improve the appearance of your terrace/s it will be immediately noticed and neighbours and passers-by will start to make positive comments and perhaps ask why and how you have made the changes and how they can start to do something similar.
If you are a groupie person or would welcome more local contacts, consider suggesting that you jointly start a local apartment gardening group or circle with a common interest in improving their living environment and the appearance of the block of apartments, enclosed community or neighbourhood.

   If there are sufficient people interested in growing a selection of seasonal vegetables on their terraces and balconies, a growing circle could be established. This may be of particular interest and benefit in apartment blocks and communities where there is a high percentage of single tenants.

1.11 Overcoming the Potential Problems

A. PLANTS DRYING OUT

One immediate reaction when we say 'How about some colour on your terrace or balcony?' is 'We've tried but everything soon dried up and died. We could not keep up with the watering'. Unfortunately they had tried the impossible – window boxes of thirsty annuals in poor compost in the summer on a south-facing terrace in full sun. As you will discover in Part Four, there are many drought-resistant plants that would be much more appropriate and easier to maintain. Also a blind or awning installed to protect plants on the outer edge of a covered terrace from the summer sun and those near the inner wall from the low winter sun can soon pay for itself. Also Part three will explain that there are other ways of providing colour than plants.

B. MICROCLIMATE

Each apartment terrace has its own microclimate. Some are the best on the Med. Others rather harsher and less pleasant for owners and their plants. What you experience season by season will be determined by the direction your terraces and balconies face and the local pattern of windy weather. This includes direct winds, those channelled between buildings and the special phenomena of up-draughts on the sunny sides of skyscraper apartment blocks. The microclimate of a first-floor, sunny-side apartment in Benidorm can be very different to that of a north-side apartment on the 25th or even 43rd floor. In lower apartment blocks a six-storey penthouse terrace can be a combination of a hot desert with the reflected heat from the hot floor tiles and a chilly mountaintop when strong winds bounce dried-out plants in small plastic pots – only watered a few hours before – across the terrace.

But that is totally unnecessary. Larger plastic pots to hold more compost and moisture placed inside more attractive terracotta or glazed ceramic pots would immediately solve the two problems of fast drying out and stability of plant layouts.

Naturally you can use blinds, awnings, tall plants and windbreaks to combat hot suns and winds but the best solution is naturally to think about the microclimate of terraces and balconies before you buy an apartment in the first place. We know of apartments where you will see persons using the terrace at all times of the day – spring, summer, autumn and winter – and others where we have never seen anybody.

Knowing that it is not possible for everyone to purchase the ideal microclimate and that in practice some people love the sun and others prefer the shade, we include design and plant ideas for a wide range of situations as you progress through the book.

C. TIME
Timewise apartment gardening is a cinch compared to starting with a typical Mediterranean garden site with hard, poor, rocky soil full of buried builders' rubble as well as rocks, which can take years to transform into a pleasant garden retreat. Whether you opt for a simple improvement or a sophisticated interior design approach, you can achieve much in only a

day or a week, particularly if you read through this book first to clarify the best options for the size and location of your covered and open terraces and balconies before rushing out to spend money on the first idea that comes to mind.

D. CARRYING WEIGHTS

Transporting pots, plants and bags of compost can be difficult for infirm persons but there are ways to work around this.

a. Buy lightweight and/smaller containers and smaller potted plants and bags of compost.

b. Ask a garden centre to plant and transport your containers to your apartment.

c. Find a gardener who specialises in terrace gardening.

E. MONEY

It makes a lot of sense to invest in making your terrace into an outdoor space or room where you will want to spend much of your time when the weather is good and, if sheltered, also when the weather is bad. But there is no need for it to break the bank. There are sensible plants, containers, furniture, lighting effects etc. to meet all tastes and budgets.

F. MOTIVATION

Asked why they came to Spain to live, most expatriates answer 'The weather'. Yet amazingly one sees very few actively using their terraces for an outdoor extra room or persons tending their balconies and windowsills, both on the coast and in the cities. We hope that this book helps change that situation.

1.12 The Special Problems of Non-Resident Owners

Many apartments are owned by non-residents who only use them for a few weeks or months a year and in many cases let them for part of the year.

Naturally such owners don't want to invest in plants that won't survive their absences and lack of care by tenants, nor in outdoor furnishings that don't withstand wear and tear. But in many cases they would like to live in more luxury when resident.

Luckily there are plants that can survive long absences, such as succulents and cacti, and ways of improving the moisture-holding properties of composts to make this even easier. In any case it would not be unreasonable to ask tenants to water such plants once a week while asking them to water thirsty annuals twice a day is bound to fail. Even we would probably forget at times!

Plant choices are discussed in Part Four and Plant care in Part Five. Naturally you can buy thirsty plants at the beginning of each visit as if you were buying short-lifespan, cut flowers and throw or give them away at the end of your stay, or arrange for a resident neighbour friend or concierge to care for things in your absence.

Also plants do not need to be the only thing used to brighten up your terrace and turn it into an attractive outside living space. Ceramics, dried flowers, artificial plants, end wall murals etc. are all easy and not necessarily expensive alternatives. These and others are discussed in Part Three.

   We mention outdoor furniture in Part Three as it can make or break your enjoyment of siestas and wining and dining. At this point it is suffice to say: buy the most comfortable, elegant and hard-wearing you can afford and, if you let, lock away the most precious when you are away and put out something less likely to be damaged by tenants. If there is no large internal cupboard that can be locked up, a trunk or cupboard can be placed at the end of a terrace.

1.13 Let's Get Going!

Our book was designed to be read and used by all those living in an apartment. Unless living alone, let all family members read it and come up with ideas that can be discussed and prioritised before going ahead with a revamping of your currently bare terraces, balconies and even windowsills or an existing unsatisfactory design. Happy reading, making improvements and enjoying your Mediterranean living even more!

Brightening up balconies and windowsills

Ideas for making the best of balconies and windowsills, by brightening up your living and local environment with flowers, greenery and possibly a few herbs, vegetables and fruit.

2.1 The Range of Possibilities

Balconies and windowsills are by definition small or very small spaces but much more use can be made of them in many communities, villages, towns and cities to the benefit of residents as well as passers-by. As discussed in Section 1.2, rarely does one see an apartment building with more than 10 or 15 per cent of the balconies with anything on them.

An apartment block with every owner doing what they can to brighten up the entire building and street is a rare gem.

Balconies are by definition spaces cantilevered out from a building and generally to a maximum of 80cm in depth. They may only have room for a small table and a chair but one can sit in the doorway to admire one's plants in rows of pots or window boxes, step out to tend them and look up and down the street or into community gardens.

Widths can vary from the one metre width of a doorway or wall to ceiling window to the 10-metre width of an apartment. Generally they are two to five metres.

Mostly decorative flowering and evergreen plants are planted on balconies but fruit herbs and vegetables can also be productively grown as will be explained in detail in Parts Eight, Seven and Nine respectively.

All these types of plants, whether in pots or window boxes, can be hung on the top of the railings, stood on the floor or hung on the walls either side of the doorway to the balcony. On some older buildings the railings were conveniently designed with a pot/window box shelf built into them. And do recognise that window boxes can be hung on both sides of railings and that an effective mass display can be achieved by hanging opposite to each other two on the outside and two on the inside.

Windowsills are even smaller, the possibilities for growing things being restricted to the width and depth of the sill. The depth is typically 70 to 80 per cent of the thickness of the wall in which the window is inserted. But much can be grown in a space as small as 30 by 60 centimetres. Conceptually we look at windowsills as micro balconies that one can only access with hands and arms.

They exist at ground level rather than balconies and on the inner walls of balconies and terraces and on end walls of buildings.

Windowsills and balconies are two types of small spaces seen every minute of the day around the Mediterranean and indeed inland and worldwide. Unfortunately generally unused but as you will see in the next section so much can be done with them to:

a. Brighten up the outlook through the window.
b. Build up collections of plants.
c. Provide some privacy from prying eyes.

d. Brighten up the external view of your apartment whatever floor it is on to the benefit of passers-by and the occupants of apartments across the street or communal gardens.
e. Grow a few beneficial fruits, herbs and vegetables.
f. Hide eyesores seen through the window.
g. Soften the appearance of the air-conditioning unit.
h. Make the space attractive whether the blinds are down or up.

At best the combined interest and actions by the owners of all the apartments in a block can turn a very bland, uninteresting building into a veritable Hanging Gardens of Babylon. So let us demonstrate to you the possible, starting with window boxes and then moving on to balconies.

2.2 Windowsills

A. DECIDE WHAT YOU WANT

Don't just buy the first pot and plant you see and then add impulse buys higgledy-piggledy whenever you spy something eye-catching in the local market or garden centre.
Decide first whether you:

• Only want a single window box or a row of pots.
• Want coloured flowers that will require regular watering and changing several times a year or evergreen plants that need little watering and will last for years.
• Would like to experiment with growing of a few mini vegetables and fruit.
• See through the window or block it out with plants to give total privacy and perhaps shade if facing south.

B. SOME DESIGN IDEAS FOR WINDOWSILLS

Window ledges are the quickest, easiest and least expensive ways of brightening up your apartment if you have windows with sills – with or without security grills – opening on to a terrace, community gardens or the street. The best thing is to see sills as micro balconies which will look best with plants in containers.

There are two big decisions. The choice of plants and the choice of containers to house them. As illustrated in Section 4.2, there are many plants suitable for apartments and many will look fine on windowsills. The only constraints being the height of the window space, and width and depth of sill and whether the sill is exposed to hot suns and winter chills. Fortunately sills outside heated rooms have a microclimate a few degrees warmer in the winter than the street or garden due to heat losses through the glass or gaps around the window and frame. But be aware that the air emitted by air-conditioning units is warm in the winter but can be very cold in the summer and plants directly in front can suffer.

Checking through the long list of types of containers described in Part Five, the best would be a window box that fills the width of the sill or a line of suitably-sized pots. Suitably-sized pots are those that look aesthetically good when planted and are large enough to accomodate the maturing roots of plants plus sufficient compost to allow easy watering and feeding and to retain more than a day's or week's supply of moisture depending on your choice of plants. This of course can be helped by mixing a water-holding compost as explained in Section 5.4 and using non-thirsty plants.

The 12 photographs opposite illustrate the wide range of plantings that are possible, ranging from the short-lived annuals and tropical exotics to long-life solutions more practical for most people. Some are planted with seasonal plantings of annuals that will need constant watering and deadheading and changing several times a year. For instance, petunias planted in early spring need replacing by portulacas in midsummer and by pansies in the autumn to sustain a year round colourful display. Others are planted with slow-growing drought-resistant succulents that need little care including watering and can last for years – many having interesting flowers at various times of the year. Some use window boxes and others pots.

Depending on their location some of the windows show security bars and others not. In the latter case it is worth fixing a metal bar 12cm above the windowsill to prevent pots falling off in high winds!

SOME PLUSSES AND MINUSES OF EACH OF THE WINDOWSILLS.

Nº 1. Geraniums Galore
A classic sight that used to be very common in Spain until the mid-1990s when the dreaded geranium moth arrived in a contaminated importation of geraniums. Still possible if you seek out healthy plants, spray weekly with neem or a proprietary geranium moth insecticide and constantly look out for small blackening holes in the stems. These are the sign that a moth has made a hole and injected its eggs. Cut out affected branches, deadhead and remove dead leaves to keep the plants looking their best and healthy. Main problem is that neighbouring windowsills can have uncared-for, affected geraniums that are a breeding ground for the moths. Refer to Part Ten for more solutions to the problem.

Nº 2. Trailing Petunias
What a spring and summer display – and one that can last for some months if the plants are kept moist and fed with a dilute feed each week. Over-watering and feeding can lead to weak growth liable to insect and fungi attacks.

Nº 3. Mixed Petunias And Succulents
A very stimulating mix of perennial and annual plants. Both have long flowering periods if watered and mildly fed fortnightly. If deadheaded when becoming leggy, can flower again. Also an interesting combination of bright green and light green leaves.

Nº. 4. Herbs
Windowsills are a good place to establish a small collection of culinary and medicinal herbs in pots or window boxes. They look interesting, perfume the area and make productive use of the limited space. Keep trimmed by using the herbs to stop them going leggy. See Part 8.

Nº 5. Ferns

Very attractive but only practical for a windowsill that never gets direct sunlight. The plastic daisy actually adds a useful light touch. Slow growing if the compost is kept constantly damp for years.

Nº 6. Succulents

What an attractive long lasting display using a mix of succulents that will grow slowly in their small pots and need little watering. A classic planting with the plants matching the arched window.

Nº 7. A Winter Mix

Even in January there is a wide assortment of flowering plants available along the Spanish coast. There are no security bars on this windowsill so a bar 10 cm above the sill would be beneficial to stop pots from falling on windy days. Naturally this south-facing display will need regular watering even in the winter.

Nº 8. Busy Lizzies

These are many people's favourite window box plant. Can flower from spring to winter if watered and fed. Single or mixed colours can look good. Trim to keep to bushy rather than leggy shape. New plants easily raised from the cuttings.

Nº 9. Young Busy Lizzies with Herbs

Sages are combined with squat busy lizzies. A interesting blend of short and tall plants. Both should flower from the spring display shown through to the autumn if fed and watered. But both could become leggy if not deadheaded. You can also have a windowsill entirely dedicated to herbs. See Part Seven.

Nº 10. Cacti

A good choice for a windowsill that faces south with no blind to protect the plants from the hottest summer suns. Little maintenance required for years except an occasional watering and misting. The smallish pots will constrain the growth of the plants.

Nº 11. Plastic Ornaments and Leaves

Not every one's choice but, in the location we found it, it was not out of place. The plastic artefacts were apparently mementos from holidays and never needed watering but need an occasional wash to remove grime. Most people would choose a more attractive collection but it is the concept that we are illustrating. As said in the introduction, we did not set out to photograph only perfect examples and pieces set up for the photograph but rather actual arrangements that someone has been proud of.

Nº 12. Lettuces

Yes, why not. The red variety are colourful, interesting to watch grow, healthy for eating and you can cut leaves off as if they are a cut-and-come-again variety – which is another possibility. You can buy new plantlets at most times of the year to fill gaps when you eventually eat the whole lettuces. Alternatives would be oriental cut and come again salad leaves, chillies and radishes. Each could be attractive as well as productive.

▲ Filling the whole window space with flowers.   ▲ Why not mix a few vegetables in with your flowers?

In the 12 cases we have illustrated situations where window boxes and pots sitting on the windowsill have been used. However it is also possible to fill the whole window space with flowers by hanging pots at several levels on the security bars as illustrated above left. It is also possible to mix a few vegetables in with flowers as with mangetout peas above right.

Unfortunately we don't have space here for more photographs related to windowsills. However there are more photographs of possible window boxes in Section 4.5. If you need more ideas before finalising your plantings, wander round a number of neighbourhoods looking at apartment blocks and village houses. In some locations you will also notice the enormous opportunity for brightening up streets where the majority of windowsills are bare. As well as plants they can also be used for storing squash.

2.3 Balconies

A. WHAT SPACE AND WEIGHT CAPACITY DO YOU HAVE?

Naturally you have more scope for creativity on a balcony but even then it will be constrained by the dimensions and shape, and the weight-bearing limits of the method of construction and age.

Check out the latter before placing anything heavy on the balcony and prepare a sketch plan of the balcony space.

B. WHAT WOULD YOU LIKE AND WHAT IS POSSIBLE?

From the thousands of balconies we have seen we have selected nine to indicate the range of possibilities. Each is very different in its purpose and execution as discussed briefly for each balcony.

Selection of Balconies	Brief Commentary
	An exciting, south-facing traditional Spanish display of sun-loving geraniums and pelargoniums mainly in self-watering window boxes. Since the mid-1990s this type of display has become more difficult due to attacks by the geranium moth. Weekly spraying against this is required. A pity that the balcony no longer has the traditional display of coloured tiles underneath.
	Largely similar geranium plants to the previous balcony but facing east. Hydrangeas are also possible. They do not like to be exposed to hot summer suns. The pots are possible as they will dry out more slowly facing east than if they faced south. Bottom plants inside railings and outside above for denser display and privacy. Unfortunately no drip trays under pots.
	A balcony gardener. Neighbouring north-facing balconies with healthy display of over-wintering plants and interesting use of rubber and schefflera plants for height. Was the only 'green' terrace in the block.

Selection of Balconies	Brief Commentary
	Simple and effective use of a single plant and plant colour – trailing petunias. Will give a good spring and summer display but the main beneficiaries will be passers by. The residents will only see a few flowers through the window but will have reasonable privacy and the joy of seeing their apartment when returning home. Something important when one does not have a garden to walk through to the front door. Blind provides shade for room and if dropped a little also for the flowers from the hottest sun.
	Obviously an owner keen on plants and making the best of the warmer months. This terrace was in the Alpujarras coastal mountains, hot in summer with cooling breezes but very cold in the winter when this wonderful display of pelargoniums and fuchsias will not survive.
	Another mountain situation. This time in the foothills of the Pyrenees. As many mountain folk do, the owners make the best of the few warm/hot months to make homes as colourful as possible whether apartments or houses. Unfortunately often difficult to obtain this quality of trailing pelargoniums in mid and southern Spain.
	This balcony faces south and is in the dappled shade and shelter of the large leaves of a plain tree in summer and even by heavy branches in winter. Taking advantage of the shade to grow several varieties of evergreen cascading ivy to give privacy. Self-watering window boxes with built-in reservoirs being used to reduce chance of drying out and drips onto passageway below.

Selection of Balconies	Brief Commentary
	A fifth-floor balcony on an old apartment block. Owners are obviously proud of their mature collection of plants. The balcony is eye-catching, provides privacy from passers by below and neighbours opposite and improves the general appearance of the building. All the plants are in medium-sized pots except for one of the new plastic ones which mar the overall impact of the terrace.
	A sensible use of medium-sized pots with drip trays to reduce the chance of water dripping below. If sprayed weekly the geraniums, being high up, have a good chance of escaping the geranium moth.
	Facing east, these plants suffered little from the hottest suns last summer. Also used to store the squashes from the family allotment for winter eating.This photograph was taken in December. It had been a mass of colour throughout the summer.
	East-facing, striking and sophisticated, using just two sizeable yuccas and no flowering plants. Therefore very different to the others in the series. Alternatives could be well-trimmed bay, pittosporum, cupresses and citrus trees. The latter also being attractive for their flowers, perfume and fruit. Other miniature fruit trees could also be used.
	If you are an absentee owner only visiting for a few weeks a year or infirm and just can't cope with transporting heavy pots, bags of composts etc. good-looking plastic plants can have their place.

Selection of Balconies	Brief Commentary
	Facing east and receiving only the morning sun, this terrace has a mix of plants that like and dislike the hot sun. Wisely, plants have not been placed in front of the air exit from the air-conditioning unit as this blows cold in the summer and hot in the winter. The plants on top are new replacements hence less mature than the other plants. Cacti or succulents would have been a better choice for this situation.

There is a general message from this series of balconies and the many poorer ones we photographed. More plants are easier to keep on west and east-facing balconies than on ones facing due south or north. For this reason we list separately in Section 4.2 those plants happy in full midday sun and those that like less sun.

Also there are few people who yet grow vegetables on their balconies and windowsills, although this practice is becoming more popular in the cities.
We discuss this in Part Nine.

2.4. Choosing Your Plants and Containers

As you can see there are many types of plants and shapes sizes and colours of containers available. We describe some 140 plants/plant families for you to choose from in Section 4.2 and present an A to Z of containers in Part Six. In practice you can choose your plants and then look for containers or choose your containers first bearing in mind the shape and size of the windowsill or balcony.

2.5 Planting Up Your Plants

The success of your displays will depend on the choice of plants and how you care for them but even more so by the way you plant them up. This is covered in depth in Part Five but at this stage we provide you with a basic guide.

Planting up your Plants

Step 1: Digging a hole with a trowel

Step 2: Taking plant from pot

Step 3: Loosening outer roots

Step 4: Placing in hole

Step 5: Firming soil up to level of compost in pot

Step 6: Giving plant first watering

How to care for your windowsill and balcony plants is covered in detail in Part Five.

Attractive and productive terrace living spaces

There are an amazing number of ways of laying out and utilising the relatively small amount of space available on small, medium and large apartment terraces. You can lay them out for beauty, comfort, relaxation, wining and dining and privacy and also include facilities for growing healthy vegetables and fruit on a mini scale. Outlined here are basic and more creative ideas for terraces from as small as five to 15 square metres to a penthouse roof of 100 to 500 square metres.

3.1 The Range of Possibilities

The practical possibilities for improving the utilisation and enjoyment of your apartment terraces are endless whether covered or open. They range from a simple speedy brightening up this weekend by installing a few sensibly planted window boxes and a few pots to a major project taking a month or two. A project to create a stimulating and relaxing outdoor living space that challenges the accommodation inside the apartment for use and occupancy at most times of the year.

In addition, a terrace can produce a significant amount of the herbs vegetables and fruit consumed by the household.

The most important criterion for deciding what to do is 'Will it improve the lifestyle health and satisfaction of the resident owner or tenant, current or future?' The latter may be important if you want to sell.

3.2 First, What do You Want?

Before doing anything think about what you really want to do with your balcony and/or terraces. We include balconies, although discussed in Part Two, to make a comparison as many readers will have both balconies and terraces and will need to decide what to do with each.

Don't just buy the first pot and plant you see and then add impulse buys higgledy-piggledy when ever you spy something eye-catching in the local market, garden centre or ceramic shop. Decide first what you want.

The following are two possibilities.

- Place a few window boxes or pots or improve existing ones to add a little stimulating or restful colour and improve the image of the property from the street of community gardens.

- Transform an under-utilised terrace space into an exciting outdoor living area that could become where you spend most of your time when at home.

But there are many others. The table opposite summarises various statements of personal needs shared with us by expatriates and Spaniards interested in or already living in apartments.

All those needs are realistic and feasible provided you have the space . But most will not have. The lucky ones will be those with a large terrace – perhaps a penthouse terrace - particularly if half is open and half covered.

So priorities will need to be set. We suggest that you read through the list of 'what you want' carefully and tick those that match your aspirations and add any others that come to

WHAT DO YOU WANT? Typical needs include the following	Balcony	Small/ medium -sized terrrace	Large terrace
1. Just have some plants	✓	✓	✓
2. Have 12 months of colour	✓	✓	✓
3. Have some romantic perfume	✓	✓	✓
4. Some evergreen plants would be nice	✓	✓	✓
5. Be able to sit out in the sun	✓*	✓	✓
6. But must have shade at times	✓	✓	✓
7. Able to eat out at all times of day		✓	✓
8. It would be nice to be able to entertain friends		✓	✓
9. Keep the wonderful views we have	✓	✓	✓
10. Privacy when we are eating or sunbathing		✓	✓
11. Display collection of artefacts		✓	✓
12. To have a perpetual-fruiting lemon tree and perhaps a grape vine, perhaps a few other trees	✓*	✓	✓
13. To grow a few vegetables	✓*	✓	✓
14. The relaxing sound of water, and we miss the garden pond and fountain we had		✓	✓
15. Have somewhere to meditate		✓	✓
16. Space for hobbies		✓	✓
17. Space for games			✓
18. To be able to glaze us in during the winter and storms		✓	
19. A jacuzzi if it would fit in			✓
20. Storage space for things when we let etc.		✓	✓
21. To have a song bird or two	✓	✓	✓
22. To have a laying hen	✓*	✓	✓
23. Space for you to write your own			
24.			
25.			
26.			
27.			
28.			

* Possible but limited compared to a terrace

mind as the list is not all-inclusive. If you are a family, it makes sense to involve everybody in the process.

Then go back and set some priorities by marking up each of the objectives you ticked with:

E Absolutely essential could not live without.

I Important would not like to be without.

L Would like if can fit in but if not could live without.

This is important as you will want to enjoy your apartment terraces to the maximum but still be able to move around. So, when you measure and check the shape of the terraces of your existing or new apartment, some things will just not fit in unless you drop other requirements in exchange. We will look at some possible designs for small, medium and large-sized terraces in the sections that follow. Beyond these designs we consider how best to locate plants on terraces and how to improve the microclimate and ambience of terraces in general.

As you review each of them ask yourself;
- Could you live in it?
- Does it look comfortable?
- Is it colourful?
- Is it restful?
- Does it make good use of the available space?
- Does it have privacy?
- Is there sun and shade?
- Would it need much maintenance?
- Can you imagine yourself relaxing and wining and dining there?
- Is it better than what you have?

3.3 Some Design Ideas for Small Terraces

We regard terraces of up to 10 square metres as small. The imperatives are to keep things simple and make use of every square centimetre of space without cluttering the terrace. Three very different styles are illustrated opposite and discussed below.

❶ A 10-SQUARE-METRE COVERED TERRACE

Photograph 1 shows a garden in the sky, six stories up in an otherwise unattractive apartment block. The owners were obviously determined to sit out on as 'green' a terrace as possible. They could not have fitted many more plants in.

The trellis panel is covered in climbers to act as a wind break. They are using the traditional pot and window box supports built into the railings for a mix of plants to brighten

DESIGN IDEAS FOR SMALL TERRACES

the terrace and provide privacy. There also plants in wall-hanging pots. One can pick out ivy, ferns, tradescantias, dipladenias, ficus bengamini, epiphylum. All included in the 100-plus sensible plants for terraces included in Section 4.2.

❷ A SIX-SQUARE-METRE TERRACE

Photographs 3 and 4 illustrate a quick makeover of a terrace only six square metres in size - 3 x 2 metres. The terrace was initially little used except for some sunbathing in spite of the exceptional view because it faced due south. In summer it could become an oven with the direct sunlight and reflected heat off three walls and hot terracotta floor tiles. But there was an enviable view.

The simple act of installing a roll-out awning changed everything as there was then shade on the terrace and in the study bedroom. With shade the terrace was soon converted into an attractive, low-maintenance, simply furnished terrace that could be used to work, quietly read and have cosy meals.

The simple plan consisted of:

- A sun awning rolling out from the back wall for sunny days and to make the terrace cosy for dining on cloudy nights. The photographs were taken early on a December morning when the low sun came into the terrace but by lunch time it would be beating down on the awning as it would all summer.

- Small collections of low-maintenance, drought-resistant succulents in the two front corners between the side walls and the balustrade wall. The shade behind the latter helped keep the roots of the plants cool.
- No window boxes on the balustrade wall in order to take advantage of the natural view.
- Retaining the old 95cm diameter table but covering it with a bright Bolivian cloth and purchasing new, better-looking, more comfortable seats. Two are shown and two for visitors are stored in a corner.
- The inner wall brightened by two succulents in coloured wall-hanging pots and a perpetual lemon tree in an attractive, Spanish-style, decorated tub in the inner right-hand corner.

Exactly the same plan could be used for a same-sized terrace with a ceiling. In this case we would recommend a pull-down blind to give shade from the low winter sun and a painting or ceramic mural could be placed on one side wall.

❸ A 10-SQUARE-METRE OPEN TERRACE

The photographs 5 and 6 show an open terrace of only four metres length by two-and-a-half-metres wide as used during the day and evening.

The initial objectives had been to:

- Establish a collection of drought-resistant succulents that requires little maintenance and creates a green space.
- Enable day-time vitamin D sunbathing and lunch-time and evening dining.
- Hide away the tools and ecological plant feeds and insecticides.
- Keep the central floor space uncluttered .

The photographs show the terrace that evolved as seen in the middle of the day and in late evening. The only differences layout-wise between the two photographs are that;

a. the folded table stacked at back left in the first photograph has swapped places with the now-folded sun bed, and

b. the two chairs at the table in the daytime are now stored unseen alongside the entrance door to the terrace.

A significant collection of small and medium-sized succulent plants lines the outer edges of the terrace on all four sides. They are planted in a variety of terracotta pots with the exception of two in ceramic pots on the trolley and four in ceramic wall pots on the unseen left hand wall.

Two plants are housed in a now-unused Mexican oven previously used in a villa garden but neighbours to the apartment would not welcome the hot air smoke and odours. So tagines on small charcoal heaters are now used for alfresco cooking.

The plastic storage box on the bottom shelf of the trolley is in fact the 'garden shed'. Use of floor space is maximised, it could hardly be greener and the maintenance is low. Some may say "chic" others "cluttered" but the book is designed to present a wide range of possibilities for all tastes.

❹ A FOUR-SQUARE-METRE ALLOTMENT TERRACE

More and more people are starting to grow vegetables in containers that take up little space. This is being done at the end or in corner of terraces, or by dedicating an entire small terrace to vegetable-growing.

The photograph shows a four square 1.5 by 2.5 metre terrace being set up as a mini allotment or *huerto urbano* as it would be called in Spanish.

A later photograph of the terrace when planted is shown in section 9.1 C (page 169). Part Nine explains the many ways of growing vegetables on terraces, balconies and even windowsills.

A plan for establishing a mini orchard of nine fruit trees on a same-sized terrace will be found in Part Eight. Small can be bountiful as well as beautiful!

3.4 Some Ideas for Medium-Sized Terraces

In this section we illustrate five very different medium-sized terraces which are illustrated in the photographs on the next page.

❶ ❷ ❸ A 12-SQUARE-METRE COVERED TERRACE

The terrace shown in photograph 1 was essentially designed for reading, eating all meals and having a sundowner with tapas all the year round, surrounded by a collection of perennial plants.

SOME IDEAS FOR MEDIUM-SIZED TERRACES

Shortly after this photograph was taken a bag for growing wild mushrooms was slid amongst the plants – see photograph 3.

The glazed, west-end, arched window provides year-round shelter from wind and rain. Although not a large, terrace eight people can be seated at the table and the sunblind is used to shade people sitting to eat on a space-saving bench seat set against the railings as shown in photograph 2. In the winter the sunblind is used to protect the inner shade-loving plants from the low winter sun that comes right into the terrace. In the summer it is too high to bother plants.

The right wall is partially decorated with country antiquities and a pair of budgies chirp away in a large cage on the end wall. Overall a homely terrace.

④ A 12-SQUARE-METRE TERRACE.

Photograph 4 is a peep at a long, narrow, 8-by-1.5 metre terrace festooned with geraniums in flower throughout the year. They are hung on the railings and placed on sideboards at either end of the tastefully furnished terrace.

Walls and furniture are white. The terrace is the only one really cared for in a block of a hundred apartments. One of the residents was a prominent member of a gardening club inn England before retiring but what is done is achievable by all inexpensively.

The main challenge is keeping the geranium months at bay by regular spraying – see Part Ten.

⑤ A 15-SQUARE-METRE SHADED TERRACE

Photograph 5 shows a very different style to the others. Perched high up in a southern city centre surrounded by eyesores and potentially an oven in the summer.
The owners chose to go for privacy and shade but with sufficient light to allow climbers to grow on the trellis. An attractive hideaway from the local hustle and bustle.

⑥ A 20-SQUARE-METRE TERRACE

Photograph 6 shows an open terrace shaded by a folding awning on wires with attractive terrace views. Clinical and simple and not a gardener's terrace. But sufficient plants in pots to make it intimate and interesting. Could be a terrace on the slope of a pyramid block or the top terrace of a small block.

⑦ A 20-SQUARE-METRE OPEN TERRACE

Photograph 7 shows the ground floor courtyard or patio terrace of a four-storey apartment building. The occupants of the two ground-floor apartments have the use of the courtyard terrace with the occupants of the apartments above having the benefit of the colour of the plants including climbers up to the upper floors.

However the courtyard lacks privacy as it is overlooked. Therefore it is just used to build up a plant collection and not for eating out.

3.5 Some Design Ideas for Large Terraces

We often look up at the tops of apartment buildings and seeing signs of plants wonder what is up there.

All we know in most cases is that there are sizeable roof-top terraces of 50 to several hundred square metres which open up all sorts of opportunities. But there are two drawbacks that need to be tackled for comfort – the provision of shade from sunrise to sunset and protection from howling winds.

We illustrate and comment on three typical situations and then suggest ideas for a dream terrace.

A. A HALF-OPEN ATICO-STYLE ROOF GARDEN

Some top-floor *ático* terraces have an open sunny area and an area semi-shaded by an upper beam structure integral with the building. The latter is often not exposed to prevailing winds or direct sunlight and therefore suitable for a colourful area. The photograph shows the 60-square-metre semi and deeper-shaded area of a plant-lover's 200-square-metre roof-top. Yes, definitely for resident rather than holidaying owners. Obviously a plant lovers hidden garden. The construction of the apartment provided for an area sheltered from howling winds and the owners have maximised it's use.

B. OPEN ROOF-TOP TERRACE

This open 100-square-metre terrace has immediate impact. Many will say 'We would love that'. It can be summed up as: 'Chic, stylish, partly shaded with fixed shade, interesting plants – including a lemon tree off to the right, good choice of pots in shape colour and size – except the climbing bougainvilleas would be better in larger pots, comfortable furniture, trellis for climbing plants and good sea view. If you look carefully you will notice that the trellis

is backed by glass to provide a wind break without interrupting the distant views. Unseen there are sun-loungers and we would have added an area for growing vegetables and herbs and possibly a succulent collection.

Luckily the pots chosen are heavy enough not to blow over in a gale. When we stepped out on the terrace of another penthouse terrace, herbs in smallish dried-out plastic pots had scuttled across the terrace with only a light breeze.

A very Mediterranean choice of plants most not being thirsty plants. They include oleanders, lavender, palms, a lemon tree and bougainvilleas.

C. A MORE ECONOMIC START

Just getting going with a 150-square-metre rooftop terrace. Some sensible plants and pots but a blind on the south side of the gazebo would ensure day time shade on the hottest days and some protection from winds.

D. 'DREAM' HOLISTIC PENTHOUSE GARDEN PLAN

We have searched around for a fully developed holistic penthouse terrace that would satisfy our needs should we win one of the major national lotteries. In preparing the book we have seen totally bare ones, the owners having purchased the penthouse as an investment but being too busy workwise to do anything with it. Others were partially developed when owners moved into sheltered accommodation or passed away. In many cases the rooftop terrace was not much used as there was little shelter from the sun and winds. So we found no ideal terrace for our purpose. We knew that no one these days could afford a rooftop garden the scale of the Rooftop Spanish Garden in London or the amazing rooftop cacti garden in Gran Canarias so we took a different approach.

We drew up a more modest practical and affordable plan for a 'Dream Terrace' should we ever win the lottery. A layout that could satisfy our life-style needs and enable us to achieve a holistic garden in the sky that grew flowers, herbs, fruit and vegetables with sunny and sheltered areas, enclosed areas within climber-clad trellis work screens and open areas to see the long distant sea and mountain views.

The start point was to crystallise our vision in a modified version of the holistic garden chart included in our earlier sister books *Growing Healthy Fruit in Spain* and *Growing Healthy Vegetables in Spain* and the garden lifestyle questionnaire of *Your garden in Spain*.

The plan below is our practical conversion of that strategic vision into what we will create should the dream bank transfer arrive.

HOLISTIC CHART

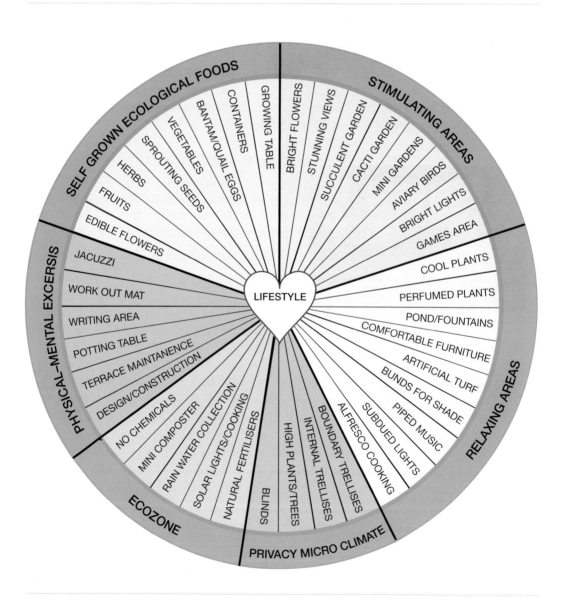

DREAM ROOF TOP GARDEN PLAN

The frame work of the plan is four mini gardens separated by 'green' windbreaks dedicated to keeping fit, eating well, growing fruit and vegetables, meditating and enjoying the distant views.

The main features are:

1. Dining in enclosed herb garden under expanding gazebo with awning on wires. Perfumed and colourful climbers such as jasmine, a trained lady of the night and stephanotis on trellis and end wall. Herb collection in planters attached to trellis except in front of sliding doors. See Part Seven for possibilities. Arch out to other areas.
S = Solar cooker; M = Mexican oven. WT = Water tank

2. Growing vegetables on growing tables. Area protected from north winds by trimmed hedging plants such as pittosporum or bottlebrush, growing in troughs with trellis attached. WT = Water tank; G = Green house; S =Shed; T = Growing tables.

3. Mini orchard with collection of fruit trees and vines growing in tubs and three wild strawberry barrels. See possibilities in Part Eight. Fr = Fruit tree; P = flowering plants in containers e.g. geraniums, portulacas and petunias; T = table.

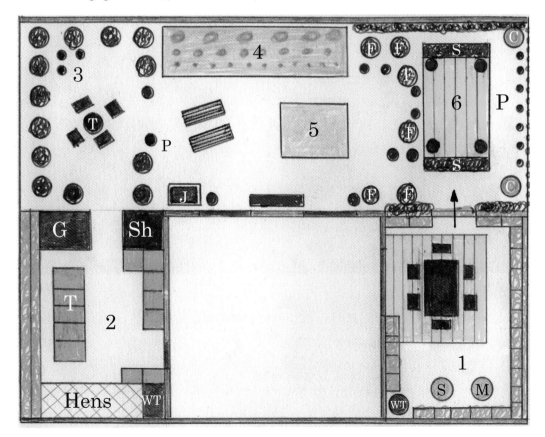

4. Cacti and succulent collection incorporating a water feature. Large cacti at back set off against mural of desert and sky.

5. Sunning and exercise area incorporating a jacuzzi, exercise mat and sun beds.
Area brighten up by colourful plants in containers including low-growing lantanas, plumbago, pineapple and velvet sages, margaritas and leonotis.

6. Sheltered relaxing area with a gazebo with a sliding awning on wires surrounded by succulents, flowering plants and flowering trees in containers. Plantings along the railings would be a collection of flowering succulents and geraniums. Bougainvilleas, mandevillas and passion flowers would be trained up the corner posts of the gazebo and end wall. The best – almost southerly view – is through the railings so relaxing rain-resistant settees and seats will be placed under the gazebo. F = flowering trees; S = Succulents in troughs. C = Cordylines. P = Flowering plants in pots

Overall an attractive and productive use of the 400 square metres of terrace surrounding 120 square metres of rooms.

Having illustrated what is possible for all sizes of terraces the sections that follow 3.6 'Communal Areas' will provide ideas for improving your new designs and existing terrace layouts.

3.6 Communal Areas

Some apartment blocks have communal areas external to apartments that can be brightened up by a single apartment owner, a few neighbours or a community 'gardening circle' with or without the community gardener.

1. The railings or balustrades of external steel or concrete staircases.

2. Pots or window boxes on the outside wall of a passageway along a long balcony to apartment entrances.

3. A common, shady, entrance lobby to two or four apartments off a long gallery running the length of the building. These might be open or closed at the end.

4. A shady passageway between the end walls of two apartments the entrance doors to both being to the right and left beyond the passageway.

5. The gardens either side of gardens running between blocks.

3.7 Locating Plants Effectively

In the photographs you have seen so far plants and the way they are displayed have been important. We therefore present practical ways for displaying them to maximise their impact and at the same time minimise the floor space they will take up.

a. Hanging on balustrades or railings in pots or window boxes to give the sense of being in a garden with some privacy especially when sitting down – but this can cut out important views. If you are short of space, pots and window boxes can be hung on the outside rather than inside of railings or balustrades. Pots and window boxes with drip trays are best in both situations. A block of four window boxes with two hanging on the outside and two hanging opposite can make an impressive display.

b. Hanging on walls in sealed terracotta or ceramic hanging pots, or a wall pouch unit to create a green wall. Colourful but constant watering!

c. Lining the outside of the floor area in pots, window box size troughs, tubs or troughs.

d. If you are interested in climbers these are best supported by wires or trellis on walls and the terrace railings. In both cases they are best planted in corner containers or a planter with attached trelliswork.

e. A vigorous evergreen pothos trained and supported across the ceiling from a corner container.

f. On wall shelf units, illustrated on the next page.

g. Trailing plants can be interestingly displayed in hanging pots – but not where one can continually bump into them. Place at the outer edge or high up to avoid this. Hanging pots make more sense than hanging baskets in most situations in a hot climate as the latter dry out quickly during the hottest times of the year. Many other novel ways of planting vegetables are included in Part Nine.

h. A particularly attractive plant in the centre of the terrace table.

i. Specimen plants can be raised up for effect on terracotta and ceramic plinths,

▲ Low in maintenance!　　　　　▲ Very space saving!

▲ Easily knocked up

upturned flower pots and small tables.

j. Small collections can be effectively displayed on tables, growing tables and plant pot theatres/steps with two or three tiers.

k. Islands of plants are not recommended except on large terraces. But in this case groups of potted plants such as succulents and cacti, rockeries and water feature areas with plants and even flower beds can be very effective and easy to create.

l. A planter or trough on castor wheels planted up with thickly growing trimmed shrubs or perfumed climbers will create a moveable hedge to place:

– alongside railings for privacy while you relax or dine, or

– across a long narrow terrace to split the leisure area from the work/storage area of clothes drying, bicycle storage etc.

Climbing beans, courgettes and cucumbers could also be planted in such a planter or trough.

m. Climbers planted in a number of planters or troughs with attached trellis work can act as a permanent windbreak around the edges of terraces. On larger terraces such units can be used as internal windbreaks as well breaking up the terrace into a series of three or four mini gardens in the style of the 12 mini gardens of the Trianan Palace in Cordoba but on a much smaller scale. In this case trellis arches can be fitted into the trellis windbreaks. See a possible plan on page 51.

The Onopiu catalogue includes the most comprehensive range of planter/trellis products and suggested layouts that we have come across for terraces. See page 57.

n. Herbs and vegetables can be grown in pots troughs, planters and growing tables. See Parts Seven and Nine.

o. Flowering and fruiting trees can live well in pots and tubs. See Part Eight.

p. Small pots of succulents and leeks can be supported on a down pipe or concrete column to make it interesting. Likewise painted beer cans can be fixed to a strip of wood or threaded on wire to house small succulents. See centre photograph on page 53.

The full range of plant containers are described in Part Six to help you select the best for your specific apartment terrace.

Before you finalise your planting plan or your current terrace becomes over-full with plants do recognise that every plant has to be watered and otherwise cared for whether you have one or a hundred.

3.8. Improving the Terrace Environment

In this section we discuss a number of things that can be done to improve the microclimate and comfort of a terrace for the benefit of both plants and people. Some are relevant to covered terraces, others to open terraces and some to both. Some decorative alternatives to plants are included in Section 3.9.

A. AWNINGS AND BLINDS

Awnings and blinds are essential for giving shade to both people and plants. In the summer they provide shelter from the hottest hours of the high sun and in the winter from the low sun reaching into the back of covered terraces. They are also attractive as illustrated. Fortunately on some apartment blocks they were installed as part of the initial fitting out with community rules requiring that all remain identical. In other situations a wide choice of fabrics are available and for smaller terraces and balconies wooden and plastic blinds are practical alternatives.

▲ Open terrace awning　　▲ Closed terrace awning　　▲ Wooden blind

B. GAZEBOES

As illustrated on page 49 metal and wooden gazeboes can be attractive, giving support for perfumed climbing plants as well as shade. They can be purchased from specialists, constructed by local blacksmiths or carpenters or DIY. Curtained gazebos are frequently seen in gardens and ground floor terraces. However, although attractive, they do need to be fixed firmly to the ground on high, windy terraces and the fabric can tear in high winds.

C. TRELLIS WORK

Trellis panels are useful for supporting plants on all sizes of terraces for supporting plants and providing a degree of privacy if attached to front railings and balustrades. However they really become essential on rooftop terraces to create windbreaks around the outer edges and to create colourful internal windbreaks around mini garden areas. For these purposes trellis attached to planters and seats plus arches are now available and are used in the Dream Terrace design on page 51. The best selection we know of is in the Unopiu catalogue as illustrated by these two units above.

C. MOBILE HEDGES

Planters and troughs on castors – with or without attached trellis panels – can be planted with trimmed evergreen or flowering shrubs or climbers to create moveable hedges.
The planters being moved from place to place to:

* Provide privacy.
* Act as a windbreak.
* Hide the end or corner of a terrace where things are stored or the drying frame/clothes line is used on washdays.

D. GLAZING

There has been a trend in some areas to install frameless sliding glass walls and permanent double glazing to part or the entire open side/s of a covered terrace. There are advantages and disadvantages to this in relation to plants.

Advantages:

a. Plants can be protected from driving rain and gales at all times of the year.

b. A glazed terrace becomes a greenhouse in the winter so tender plants can be protected, seeds started and winter tomatoes grown.

c. In most cases the original balustrade or railings are retained so window boxes and pots can still be hung on the outside.

Disadvantages:

a. If the glazing is floor to ceiling it is not possible to hang window boxes and pots on the inside.

b. If south-facing it will become very hot when closed up so if you plan to be away for long periods only cacti and succulents in large pots will survive without an automatic irrigation system. Hozelock market a suitable system.

If you are only likely to be away for weeks rather than months, bags of water-retaining gel can be placed on the surface of the compost and drip-watering heads can be screwed on empty plastic water or soft drink bottles that are upturned and pushed into the surface of the compost. You can also make a mini watering system by connecting a garden irrigation system drip head to a length of small bore irrigation tubing with a five-litre water bottle acting as a water reservoir.

E. HEATING THE TERRACE

Having created an enviable terrace it's a shame when it cannot be used on chilly days especially during the autumn and winter. An infrared or gas terrace heater may therefore be of interest.

F. PIPED MUSIC

Favourite mood music can enhance a restful or fiesta day or evening on the terrace. Loudspeakers can be hidden among the plants and the more sophisticated terrace heaters now incorporate speakers and coloured mood light in the heater support.

G. TERRACE LIGHTING

Subtle wall lights set off by attractive terracotta, ceramic or old roof-tiles or lights amongst the plants can create some special evening and night-time effects. Solar lamps are not yet really powerful enough for gardens but they can be more successful when used on terraces. There are now high-tech plant tubs with a double semi-transparent skin that have lights in between so that the container glows and light up surrounding plants. Also large stones that glow at night. Both are recharged by mini solar panels.

H. COMFORTABLE FURNITURE

Uncomfortable furniture can cause a terrace not to be used more than a lack of style in the design. So ensure that comfort of sun beds, rocking chairs, and dining table chairs make you want to stay enjoying the terrace environment and views instead of going inside to the sofa and television. Indeed so comfortable that the television gets moved outside for the hotter months of the year.

We find that there is no correlation between price and comfort. It would seem that some designers never actually get to sit on their creations. Perhaps it's assumed that a cushion covers up anything. But it doesn't and indeed, can make it worse.

Having found comfortable seats, decide on a stylish table to match rather than the other way around. A table that is not the exact style or colour you want can always be covered with a wipeable cloth that fits in with the overall terrace colour scheme.

Bulky comfortable seats can look well on large terraces but go for slim line designs for smaller ones. On a large terrace a swing seat with awning can be a lovely luxury.

Frequently clothes dryers take up too much space when used on small terraces and are the cause of many terraces not having flowers, tables and chairs. A high wall or ceiling model will solve the problem and plants can be hung on it when not in use.

I. STORAGE FACILITIES

Open terraces need somewhere to store summer furniture and cushions, even in the summer should it rain, and many terraces collect a degree of clutter. A smart-looking shed, a metre or two of glazed terrace space or waterproof trunk would be a wise investment. A shed storing furniture, gardening and beach things, bicycles, fishing and diving gear etc. can be easily disguised with climbing or hanging plants.

J. WATER FEATURES

Even for the smallest terrace there are now miniature water features available that add a special magic to small spaces, especially at night. For the larger terrace traditional fountains and fish ponds are feasible.

Aquariums can also be restful and stimulating features. They can be set on stands, tables or walls and even set into the wall of the apartment so that the fish can be seen from both the terrace and from an inside room. We have also seen terrapin ponds on terraces.

K. JACUZZI

Jacuzzis have now become very feasible even for small terraces. Lightweight portable units

now take up less than a square metre so are easily transported in a lift. Large units for high terraces require expensive cranes or even helicopters for installation.

L. FACILITIES FOR ALFRESCO COOKING

Outdoor cooking and eating can be enjoyed on even the smallest terrace and the cooking can also be done on a balcony for eating in the doorway or inside. The most practical methods of cooking are as follows:

For covered and open terraces:

• An electrically heated griddle plate. These days they can be used without oil.

• A fondue, raclette or hot stone cooker.

• A tagine or two heated on small charcoal burner/s.

For open terraces:

• A parabolic solar cooker. Interestingly the Andalusia government offered grants in 2009 for the purchase of the type of cooker shown in the photograph. They used to need one-and-a-half metres of space but a new model has reduced this to a metre. However the capacity is obviously less than the original larger one.

• A gas barbecue but in many situations the use is environmentally anti-social.

• There are a few lucky apartment owners in villages who have large back terraces with a Spanish-style outside kitchen, housing facilities for cooking in a wood-fired oven, making paellas and roasting suckling pigs.

M. BIRD TABLE AND FEEDER

A bird table for food scraps and/or a seed feeder fixed to a balustrade or railings will attract native birds including unusual migratory birds and in some areas escaped budgerigars and parakeets. Something of interest especially to children and the elderly and infirm.

N. TWO HENS FOR EGGS

We would not have included this as a serious suggestion had we not travelled six hours President class on an AVE train sitting next to an elegant lady who took her pet hen out of a basket to feed it at lunch time. It had spent two weeks on holiday with her in Córdoba and

was travelling back to it's terrace run six stories up in the centre of Barcelona. A genuine intelligent pet that delivered a fresh egg for breakfast. What better way of having a reminder of the countryside on your terrace. We therefore include two Zeebrite fantasia bantam hens in our 'Dream terrace design' on page 51.

If hens don't appeal to you, there are now attractive large cages and aviaries for budgerigars and canaries which are good pets for small spaces.

3.9 Useful Alternatives and Additions to Plants

We recognise that active terrace gardeners who want more than plants and irregular residents and busy people who don't want to be bothered with a lot of plants still want to turn a bland, inhospitable, bare terrace into a comfortable, inspiring and restful outdoor living space. We therefore consider some attractive alternatives and additions to plants recognising that some are more practical for covered versus open terraces and large versus small terraces. The most precious can be stored indoors during absences.

A. SPECIMEN CERAMIC POTS OR COLLECTIONS

There are plenty of attractive pots that look attractive individually or in groups without being filled with plants. But they can make smaller terraces looked cluttered. Look out for interesting shapes and colours. A wide range of local styles of plates are also available for hanging on walls.

B. MURALS – CERAMIC AND PAINTED

Many ceramic shops/galleries have a range of traditional tiled murals for sale and also take on commissions. They can look attractive on both covered and open terraces.

Painted murals can be done by anyone with a little artistic talent. They can be painted directly onto the wall or on a large sheet of chipboard as illustrated in the before and after photographs below.

A mural-style wall painting with a definite deep perspective will create an optical illusion that makes a terrace appear to be larger than it really is. The murals can also be painted on chipboard and fixed to the wall.

It took only three hours to transform the end of a narrow, 1.5-metre-wide terrace, including painting a mural, visiting a garden centre and hanging the first window box.

▲ Before   ▲ Soon after

C. MIRRORS

A large mirror hung on an end wall with plants in front showing a reflection of the plants and most of the terrace beyond can create an illusion that the area of the terrace is up to twice as large.

D. WALL FINISHES

Traditional white rendered walls still give an impression of space and coolness but there are others worth considering.

Tiles and panelling

There are three attractive possibilities apart from tiled murals:

a. Tile the bottom 50 cm to one metre of the walls with an attractive style and colour of tiles. The traditional Mozarabic Spanish tiles used to prevent damp can be very attractive.

b. Have a collection of old tiles or your own designs of

tiles on the walls. If you are not a potter or don't have ready access to a furnace, imitation glazed tiles can be painted on white, glazed tiles or blocks of wood.

c. Pine or other wood panelling if allowed by community rules and regulations.

E. CEILINGS

Evergreen climbing plants such as pothos can be also trained to cover ceilings. Ceilings can also be pine-clad.

F. FLOOR COLOURS

There are many styles and colours of floor tiles to choose from. In general plain terracotta or stone tiles are most effective. The more pattern in the tiles the more the potential clash and dilution of the impact of plants. But of course, if you are an absentee apartment owner looking for a minimalist terrace, coloured patterned flour tiles may be very useful to you. Ensure that non-slip tiles are used on terraces that are likely to become wet at times.

G. ANTIQUITIES

Antique ironwork, agricultural or wood working tools and utensils, and kitchenware can create fascinating wall and floor displays.

H. SCULPTURES/CARVINGS/ORNAMENTS

Sculptures, carvings and ceramic ornaments can be used to add style but can overcrowd a small terrace. They can be supported on walls, stood on plinths or the ground , stood in corners or among groups of plants and on tables or sideboards.

I. SUNDIALS

Sundials can be interesting to all ages. They can be found in an amazing number of styles. Some can be hung on a wall or balcony/terrace railing. Others can be located as stand-alone artistic pieces on large terraces, or built in as on page 60.

J. COMPASS DISPLAYS

If you have a balcony or terrace with a great distant view, why not make up a horizontal plate fixed to the railings showing the signs of the compass and the interesting things that can be seen with arrows and distances? This could start of as a self-made wooden display and end up as a cast bronze version.

K. ARTIFICIAL FLOWERS AND PLANTS

Artificial flowers can be useful to absentee owners and the infirm. They can brighten up.

a. High places difficult to access to water.

b. Very shady places where real plants would not survive.

They are available made in plastic, fabrics or silk. The best can look realistic, the worst an eye-sore. We had to walk up to and touch a metre-and-a-half high cacti the other day to prove that it was plastic. See Section 4.12 for more information.

3.10 The Way Ahead

We hope that the foregoing ideas have been inspiring and useful to you.

If you only intend to make some minor additions or changes to your apartment terrace/s make a check list of the things that you would like to do.

If you are stimulated to start from scratch or totally change what you have, don't rush into implementing the first terrace design that comes to mind. Rather make sketches of three possibilities. Then sit back and evaluate the good and the bad points of each. With these insights sketch out three more designs and again evaluate them. Then sketch a tentative final design based on the best ideas of earlier attempts. When you have studied the rest of the book, polish your design and start to implement it.

There is advantage in involving other occupants of the apartment whether family members, partners or other students in a student dwelling in order to take account of their desires and creative thinking.

Successful terrace, balcony and windowsill plants

An amazing number of flowering and evergreen plants suitable for growing in various types of containers on windowsills, balconies and terraces give opportunities for year-round or seasonal colour and perfume. We describe a selection of realistic and effective plants for the Spanish climate and then how to get the best out of them.

Healthy herb, fruit and vegetable plants and trees are discussed in later parts of the book.

4.1 The Wide Choice of Plants Available to You

When one looks at the plants on display in garden centres and flower shops an amazing number are suitable for growing in containers on your windowsills, balconies and terraces. We describe a practical selection of plants and plant groups in Section 4.2 and of course many of these will be available in a range of flower and leaf colours and flower sizes, as illustrated below.

Plant	Range of flower colours	Range of flower sizes	Range of leaf colours	Range of leaf shapes & sizes
Jasmine	Low	Low	Low	Low
Portulaca	High	Low	Low	Low
Pelargoniums	High	Medium	High	High
Pansies/violas	High	Medium	Low	Medium
Salvias/sages	High	High	High	High
Succulents	High	High	High	High

Some plants such as geraniums and bougainvilleas have long flowering periods while others such as the spectacular flowering epicacti and epiphyllums only flower for 24 hours, but what flowers – they are well worth waiting for patiently.

Epiphylum	Cyclamen	Portulaca	Nasturtium	Geranium
Very Short	Short	Average	Long	Very Long

Fortunately there are relatively long flowering period plants for spring/early summer summer/early autumn and late autumn/winter plantings

For instance, we plant several large pots and window boxes with annuals such as petunias in the spring, portulacas in mid summer when petunias struggle in the hottest suns and then we take out the portulacas at the end of October when past their best and replace with pansies.

Not all plants like the sun, very few the shade but many the sem-shade. So, as will be explained in Section 4.2, you will be wise to take account of the specific microclimate of each of your windowsills, balconies and terraces when choosing plants. It is possible to protect plants with blinds from the worst of the hottest, coldest and windiest weather but this does not mean that you can plant anything anywhere, as will be discussed in Section 5.5.

Do think about colour combinations. Some plants look best as a mass of a single colour flowers while others look most spectacular as a mix of colours. Some plants look best alone while others look best mixed with other types and varieties of plants. The possibilities are illustrated in Section 4.5.

Many readers will be using aromatherapeutic oils and incense sticks to add perfume to a room. These include the perfume of geraniums, jasmine and roses. Fortunately each of the these and other perfumed plants can be grown on terraces, as discussed in Section 4.6. The use of aromatic culinary and medicinal plants is discussed in Part Seven.

The heights of plants will also be important. For instance, in many cases low-growing plants including trailing plants than can hang down and hide the containers will be most effective but a tall cacti, ficus benjamina or climbing rose on either side of a balcony door will create more impact than two containers of small plants.

Annual flowering plants such as petunias and pansies require more deadheading and removal of dead leaves than perennial plants such as succulents. If you are a green-fingered person for whom gardening is your major love and for which you have plenty of time, you won't mind this but, if you are busy with a family or working full-time, you might. So recognise that some plants will require regular maintenance while others can be left alone for years except for an occasional watering.

Those living on the sea front will experience the problem of salt spray. We therefore indicate which plants can best survive such conditions in the plant descriptions in the next section.

The general habit of plants is mentioned in the tables but the final size of your plants, especially climbers and trees, will depend on the size of the plants you purchase and the size of containers in which you plant them, the frequency and severity of your pruning and the extent of your watering and feeding.

4.2 A Selection of Plants for Windowsills, Balconies and Terraces

In this section we describe a selection of plants chosen as being the most suitable for growing in a variety of containers on windowsills, balconies and covered and open terraces. Most of the plants can be grown on all four. A comprehensive guide to containers will be found in Part Five. Some larger plants and trees are included for larger terraces and this is mentioned in the plant descriptions. The size of these larger plants will be constrained by being grown in containers and some of the evergreens can be pruned into interesting topiary shapes.

The thirstiness of all the plants and trees is indicated in blue in the terms of high, medium and low. In addition, where appropriate we indicate whether they are perfumed (in orange), salt tolerant (in purple) and frost hardy (in red).

The plants are grouped under the following main headings for the convenience of readers.

A. Plants that can withstand full sun and require little watering even in the summer

B. Plants that can withstand direct sunlight but are thirsty plants and benefit from being shaded by blinds or awnings during the hottest summer hours.

C. Plants that prefer semi-shade.

D. Plants that survive in shade with some reflected light or in full shade.

E. Northern European indoor plants that can adapt to Mediterranean climate situations kept in semi-shade and regularly misted.

Because of the special challenge hanging pots and baskets present in Spain and other Mediterranean climate locations, we list the plants that are most suitable in Section F.

Each list is where appropriate subdivided into annuals, perennials, succulents, cacti etc. There are photographs with each description to help you identify the plants. Where a plant is available in a number of flower colours this is mentioned in the text.

For each plant we give the botanical and English name and the common Spanish name where this differs from the botanical name.

The plants are listed in alphabetical order by botanical name in each of the above sections. In addition a complete alphabetical listing of the plants by English name followed by the botanical and Spanish names is provided in the vocabulary and index on page 201.

A. PLANTS THAT CAN WITHSTAND FULL SUN AND NEED VERY LITTLE WATER

SUCCULENTS – Perennials from a wide group of families. We list our favourites.

AEONIUM/Aeonium/Eonio

Thick succulent stems with clusters of green leaves like rosettes. Some varieties have dark black/red leaves. Yellow flowers in winter.

Thirstiness-low. Salt tolerant.

COTYLEDON/Cotyledon

Clusters of succulent leaves. Pendular orange flowers on long stems in late summer.

Thirstiness-low. Salt tolerant.

CRASSULA MULTICAVA/Fairy crassula

Spreading with pale oval-shaped leaves. Delicate pink/white flowers on long stems winter/spring. Good trailing over side of pots or in hanging pots.

Thirstiness-med. Salt tolerant.

CRASSULA OVATA/Jade plant

Shiny green leaves with slight red edge. Autumn/spring, tiny pink, star-like flowers. Crassula Hobbit is a dwarf variety with woodier stems. There are many Crassulas – some form clumps, others bushy and others spreading.

Thirstiness- low. Salt tolerant.

ECHEVERIA/Echeveria

Rosettes of succulent leaves grow close to the ground or at the end of stems and can be multi-stemmed. Many different flowers at various times of year.

Thirstiness-low. Salt tolerant.

EUPHORBIA MILII/Crown of thorns

Semi-succulent shrub with bright green leaves. Very thorny stems. Flowers throughout the year with yellow flowers embedded in red or yellow bracts.

Thirstiness-low. Salt tolerant.

DROSANTHEMUM/Rocea ice plant/Mesem

Fine spreading stems with grey green leaves and masses of delicate pink/ purple daisy like flowers spring/summer. In garden used for ground cover but good trailing from tall pots and hanging pots.

Thirstiness-low. Salt tolerant.

DELOSPERMA/Mesembryanthemum/Mesem

More shrubby than the above and is nearly frost tolerant. Very bright red, pink or orange flowers summer to autumn. Mesem flowers open in sunlight.

Thirstiness-low. Salt tolerant.

PORTULACARIA AFRA/Elephant bush

Tiny green leaves set into woody twisted stems or tiny side branches. Also variegated variety. Almost looks like a knarled bonsai.

Thirstiness-low. Salt tolerant.

SEDUM MORGANIANUM/Donkey's tail

Delicate, interlocking fleshy leaves cascade downwards. Good in hanging baskets and tall tubs. Sometimes produce red flowers at stem tips in summer.

Thirstiness-low. Salt tolerant.

SEDUM RUBROTINCTUM/Christmas cheer

Low cascading with clusters of fat grape-like green leaves which turn a reddish brown in dry conditions. Yellow flowers in winter. Spreads by putting out roots.

Thirstiness-low. Salt resistant.

CACTI – All perennials, in small-medium-sized containers will not grow large.

ASTROPHYTUM MYRIOSTIGMA/Bishops cap/Astrofito

Round with 4-6 ribs. Lovely yellow flowers in mid-summer.

Thirstiness-low. Salt tolerant.

ECHINOCACTUS GRUSONII/Barrel cactus/Echinicactus

Round with very spiny ribs. Burnt-orange flowers emerge from the centre crown in mid-summer.

Thirstiness-low. Salt tolerant.

FEROCACTUS/Fierce cactus

Appropriately named as it is ribbed with very viscous spikes. Barrel-like in shape. Red, yellow or orange flowers emerge from the centre crown in mid-summer.

Thirstiness-low. Salt tolerant.

GYMNOCALYCIUM/Chin cactus

Looks like lots of chins. Low with spiky ribs. Tubular yellow or pink flowers in spring and summer.

Thirstiness-low. Salt tolerant.

MAMMILLARIA/Pin cushion cacti/Mamilaria

Round, columnar and clump-forming. Daisy-like flowers grow in a circle below the crown in spring and summer.

Thirstiness-low. Salt tolerant.

EPICACTUS/Epicactus

Tropical. Long, arching, trailing succulent-type stems with wavy edges that grow upwards and trail downwards. In spring exotic red/pink perfumed flowers grow out of stems, lasting a few days. Feed well when buds appear. Good in hanging pots. **Thirstiness-low.**

EPIPHYLUM OXYPETALUM/Orchid cactus/ Reina de la noche

Tropical epiphytic cacti. Long stems which flatten and widen as they grow. Exotic perfumed white flowers grow out of the side of these leaves lasting only one night. Good in tall pots.
Thirstiness-low.

ALOES – AGAVES – YUCCAS. All perennials – although they can grow large in gardens, planted in containers their size will be restricted.

AGAVE ATTENUATA/Agave attenuata

Pale green, soft, spineless wide leaves. Safer on a terrace or balcony than the 'Agave Americana' with its vicious spikes.
Thirstiness-low. Salt tolerant.

ALOE ARBORESENS/Candlelabra/Red hot poker

Thorny-edged, long, slender, succulent leaves. Striking red/orange flowers (like red hot pokers) on long, protruding stems early winter to early spring. Also grow well in semi-shade. Pull off dead leaves to leave a nice smooth trunk. **Thirstiness-low. Salt tolerant.**

YUCCA ALOIFOLIA/Spanish bayonet.

Palm-like with long swordlike leaves with sharp pointed ends. Best to cut off tips for safety. Good on a large terrace. Pull off dead leaves to leave a smooth trunk.
Thirstiness-low. Salt tolerant. Frost hardy.

YUCCA ELEPHANTIPES/ spineless yucca.

Often called 'false palm' when mature with its wide, shiny green, wide-drooping leaves. Has no sharp spikes like 'Aloifolia'. Suitable for a large terrace.
Thirstiness-low. Salt tolerant. Frost hardy.

PALMS AND CORDYLINES. Although they can grow large in gardens, container growing will keep them down to a manageable height.

CYCAS REVOLUTA/Sago palm
One of the oldest palms. Slow growing. Beautiful green feathery fronds. Large terraces only.
Thirstiness-low. Salt tolerant. Frost hardy.

PHOENIX CANARIENSIS/Canary Island date palm/Palmera de Canarias – phoenix
As a young plant can be grown on large terrace. Needs good light. Cut out lower fronds to keep its shape being careful of the spikes.
Thirstiness-low. Salt tolerant. Fairly frost hardy.

CORDYLINE AUSTRALIS/Cabbage tree/Dracaena roja
Straight woody trunk with leaves arching outwards. As they die pull off to leave long smooth trunk with new leaves emerging above. Flower when mature.
Thirstiness-low. Salt tolerant. Frost hardy.

B. PLANTS THAT CAN WITHSTAND DIRECT SUNLIGHT BUT ARE THIRSTY PLANTS – they benefit from being shaded by blinds or awnings during the hottest summer hours to slow down water evaporation.

ANNUALS

AGERATUM/ Floss flower /Agerato
Squat with blue flower heads larger than the bright roundish green leaves, flowers spring to autumn. Deadhead for continuous show of flowers.
Thirstiness-high. Frost hardy.

ANTIRRHINUM/Snapdragon/Boca de Dragon/Boca de lobo
Short lived spring annual. Grows slowly to 30cm. Named for its dragon like pink and mauve flowers. Deadhead for continuous show of flowers.
Thirstiness-high.

BEGONIA SEMPERFLORENS/Wax begonia/Begonia

Squat and bushy. In warmer situations can grow as a perennial and flowers most of the year. White, pale pink to red flowers. Leaves pale glossy green to dark green. Pinch out growing tips to encourage bushier growth. **Thirstiness–med.**

BRACTEANTHA/Strawflower/Planta de flores de papel.

Strawlike golden yellow/white flowers. Can be planted late winter to flower early spring to autumn.
Thirstiness-med. Frost hardy.

BRASSICA OLERACEA'Acephala group'/Ornamental Cabbage

Grown autumn to spring for their many colours.
Thirstiness-med. Salt tolerant. Frost hardy.

CALENDULA/Marigold/Calendula

Low and bushy. Pale green aromatic leaves. Yellow/orange flowers Deadhead to prolong flowering. In mild climates can grow as a perennial. Easy to grow from kept seeds sown early spring and early autumn.
Thirstiness–med. Perfumed. Frost hardy.

CAMPANULA/Bell flower

Bell shaped flowers mainly in blue or purple. Protect from winds. The flowers keep their colour better in a shady position. Spring and autumn
Thirstiness-med. Frost hardy.

CATHARANTHUS/Periwinckle/Vinca

Low and bushy. Dark green leaves. Star like flowers from white to dark pink. Pinch out the tips to keep it bushy. Be careful not to pinch out the new flower buds.
Thirstiness-med.

CELOSIA/Cockscomb/Celosia

Plume-like flowers – spring to early summer in many colours. Loves hot sun. Most popular varieties are dwarf.
Thirstiness–high.

DIANTHUS/Carnation-pink/Clavel

Many varieties and flower colours to choose from. Prefer to be shaded from midday sun and protected from strong winds. Mostly grown as annuals, flower spring to winter. Dead head for continuous show of colour. **Thirstiness-med.** Perfumed.

EUPHORBIA PULCHERRIMA/Poinsettia/Estrella de Navidad

Grown mainly for the Christmas season. Lovely red or cream bracts. Water from base and allow soil to dry out in between. Draughts and over-watering cause leaves to fall. **Thirstiness-med.**

PETUNIA/Petunia/Petunias

Long flowering season – early spring to late autumn. Trumpet-shaped flowers, many varieties and colours. Bushy and spreading. Don't like strong winds. Pinch out end shoots and deadhead regularly. Susceptible to aphids especially greenfly and whitefly. **Thirstiness–high.** Perfumed.

PORTULACA/Portulaca/Verdolaga

Flower early summer to late autumn. Low-spreading/trailing habit. Flowers, orange, pink, white, yellow, mixed. Flowers close at night and when cloudy. Good in tall pots and hanging pots. Can rot if over-watered. Love hot sun. **Thirstiness-med.**

TAGETE PATULA/French marigold/Tagete

Short. Single and double flowers – yellow, red and orange mix. In mild climate flowers spring to late autumn. Keep seeds and sow in pots in March and October. **Thirstiness-med.** Perfumed.

TROPAEOLUM MAJUS/Garden nasturtium/Capuchina

In cooler situations grown as a perennial. Trailing with tender stems, round green and variegated leaves. Red/orange/yellow flowers. Edible spicy leaves and flowers. Watch out for slugs and snails. Keep seeds and sow in pots in March and October. **Thirstiness-high.**

VIOLAS/Pansy/Pensamiento.

Squat plant. Many varieties and flower colours. Good early autumn to early spring plant. **Thirstiness-med. Frost hardy.**

PERENNIALS

ARGYRANTHEMUM/Marquerite/Margarita

Bushy, medium height. Flower spring and autumn to early winter. Many different colours. Deadhead regularly for continuous flowering. Prune to shape mid-winter to stop them going woody.
Thirstiness–med.

BOUGAINVILLEA MINI THAI/Dwarf bougainvillea

If you haven't got room for a climber try this smaller shrubby variety. Purple/red bracts most of the year. Susceptible to mealy bugs and whitefly if you over-water.
Thirstiness–med. Salt tolerant.

BUXUS SEMPERVIRENS/Common box/Boj

Evergreen shrub. Grown for its dense leathery green foliage. Make attractive single specimens, or can be used as a low hedge windbreak or for topiary. Dwarf variety 'Microphylla.'
Thirstiness- med. Salt tolerant. Frost hardy.

CAESALPINIA GILLIEPSII/Bird of paradise bush/Poinciana

Sub-tropical small tree. Fern-like leaves and exotic yellow flowers with red stamens in summer. Deciduous in cold climates.
Thirstiness-med. Frost hardy.

CALLISTEMON VIMINALIS/Weeping bottlebrush/Calistemon

Flowering shrub. Produces lovely, red, brush-like flowers several times a year. There are many other varieties. Control the size by pruning lightly after flowering in late winter. **Thirstiness–med. Salt tolerant. Very frost hardy.**

CESTRUM NOCTURNUM/Lady of the night/Galán de noche.

Green deciduous shrub. Thin arching branches growing from base. Late summer, autumn, pale green, highly perfumed flowers. Prune back hard in late winter. **Thirstiness–med. Perfumed. Frost hardy.**

CHRYSANTHEMUM/Chrysanthemum/Crisantemo

Perennial but often used as a winter annual. Flowers late summer and winter. Many different colours. Do not over-water and deadhead regularly for continuous flowers. **Thirstiness–med. Perfumed. Frost hardy.**

CODIAEUM VARIEGATUM/Garden croton.

Medium-sized upright plant. Grown for its coloured leaves. Dislikes fluctuating temperatures or strong winds. Would prefer some dappled shade. Stand on a tray with pebbles and water to keep up humidity in hot weather. **Thirstiness-med. Salt tolerant.**

CUPRESSOCYPARIS LEYLANDII/Leyland ciprés/Ciprés leylandi

Evergreen tree grown as single specimen or use for a hedge windbreak. Keep trimmed to shape. Fungal problems if over-watered.
Thirstiness–med. Salt tolerant. Very frost hardy.

DATURA –BRUGMANSIA/Angel's trumpet/Datura

Flowering semi-evergreen poisonous shrub (especially dangerous for animals and children). Long trumpet flowers in cream or pale pink. Could trim it to grow as a standard.
Thirstiness–med. Perfumed.

ERICA – E.gracilis/Cape heather

Although a perennial it is often treated as an annual when grown in containers. Mostly pale pink flowers autumn/winter. Do not allow soil to dry out. Acid-loving, so water with rain water. Mist in hot weather.
Thirstiness-med. Salt tolerant. Frost hardy.

EUONYMUS JAPONICUS/Spindle tree/Evonimo

Evergreen shrub with shiny dark green or variegated leaves. Keep trimmed to shape.
Thirstiness–med. Salt tolerant. Frost hardy.

EURYOPS CHRYSANTHEMOIDES/ Paris daisy//Margarita

Medium-sized evergreen shrub with yellow daisy-like flowers that flower on and off all year round, especially if you deadhead them regularly. Prune back to shape in early summer after first flowering.
Thirstiness–med. Salt tolerant. Frost hardy.

GERANIUM/Pelargonium/Geranio Nos 1-4
1.) GRAVEOLENS/Rose Geranium/Graveolens-perfumada

Bushy and trailing. Small pink flowers, upper petal flecked purple in spring. Perfume helps deter insects. Early winter trim back to shape. Scented leaves used for distilling geranium oil. **Thirstiness-med. Frost hardy.**

2.) PELTATUM/Ivy-leafed geranium/Murciana

Trailing with straggling stems. Dainty pink, red or orange flowers. Also many ivy-leafed hybrids which have larger flowers, single and double heads and many different colours. Tolerate over-watering more than other varieties. Bugs: geranium moth.

Thirstiness-med.

3.) REGAL/Regal Geranium

Woody stems, medium height, bushy growth. Attractive multiple-head flowers with many different colours. Deadhead to keep flowering. Trim to shape in late summer.

Thirstiness-med.

4.) ZONALE/Zonal Geranium

Upright with kidney-shaped leaves. Medium height. Clumps of brightly coloured flowers on long stems flower from spring through to late autumn. Deadhead to keep flowering. Susceptible to geranium moth. In seriously infested areas treat as annuals.

Thirstiness-med.

HIBISCUS ROSA SINSENSIS/Chinese hibiscus/Hibisco rosa de China

Woody shrub. Flowers spring to late autumn. Single and double flowers in many colours. Flowers last a day. In winter cut back to shape. Do not like being over-watered – prefer a fertiliser high in potassium and low in nitrogen. Susceptible to mealy bugs and aphids.

Thirstiness-med. Salt tolerant.

JUNIPER/Juniper/Junipero

Low spreading hardy conifer with needle like foliage. Look for dwarf varieties. Cut them back if they get too big.

Thirstiness-med. Salt tolerant. Frost hardy.

LAGERSTROEMIA/Crape Myrtle/Lagestroemia

Deciduous tree with clusters of deep red or pink crinkly flowers in summer. Shelter from strong winds.

Thirstiness-med. Salt tolerant.

LANTANA CAMARA/Common lantana

Woody shrub, small clusters of button-like flowers from spring to late winter. Several colour mixes. Most prolific is the red/orange, yellow the least. In growing season trim off dead flowers and seeds. If they get leggy cut back to shape. Late winter cut back by half.

Thirstiness-med. Salt tolerant.

LANTANA MONTEVIDENSIS/Trailing lantana/Lantana rastera

Trailing with pretty clusters of mauve flowers. Also white variety. Trim back to shape in winter.

Thirstiness-med. Perfumed. Salt tolerant. Frost hardy.

LAURUS/Bay/Laurel

Evergreen shrub or small tree. Smooth glossy leaves. Grows well as hedge for windbreak in a trough or planters, as a standard and for topiary. Leaves used in cooking. Susceptible to scale, mealy bug and sooty leaves.

Thirstiness-low. Salt tolerant. Frost hardy.

LEONOTIS/Lion's ear

Deciduous shrub. Striking, large orange flower summer to early winter. Deadhead to maintain flowering. Cut back by half in late winter.

Thirstiness- medium. Frost hardy.

LAVANDA/Lavender/Espliego

Many different varieties. Flower spring to late winter. Deadhead to encourage new flowers and trim back to shape when finished flowering. Dry flowers for 'pot pourri'. Do not over-water. Susceptible to mealy bug

Thirstiness-low. Perfumed. Salt tolerant.

NERIUM/Oleander/Adelfa

Evergreen, green and variegated leaves. Flowers spring and autumn. Many colours from white, cream, pink, salmon to red. Dwarf variety – Nerium Petite (Adelfa enana). Prune to shape late autumn after flowering. Susceptible to mealy bug, aphids and sooty leaves.

Thirstiness-med. Salt tolerant. Frost hardy.

PHORMIUM/New Zealand flax/Phornium.

Clump forming with long, strap-like, striped leaves with many different bright foliage colours. Good in large containers. Flowers emerge on long stems in summer. Do not allow soil to dry out in summer.
Thirstiness-med. Salt tolerant. Frost hardy.

PHYLLOSTACHYS AUREA/Fishpole bamboo/Bambú

Bamboo with dense foliage. Makes a good screen. Prefers a sheltered position.
Thirstiness-high. Salt tolerant.

PICEA PYGAMAEA/Dwarf spruce/Picea enana

Evergreen tree suitable for terraces. Keep trimmed to shape. Likes some shelter from winds. Prone to fungal infections in wet/humid situations.
Thirstiness-med. Salt tolerant. Frost hardy.

PITTOSPORUM TOBIRA/Japanese mock orange/Pitosporo

Very hardy evergreen shrub. Pale to dark green, shiny leaves. Cream-scented flowers in spring. Good windbreak. Keep trimmed. Also dwarf variety (Pittosporum enano).
Thirstiness-low. Very salt tolerant.

PLECTRANTHUS COLEOIDES/Swedish ivy/Planta de incienso

Green leaves with cream scalloped edges. Good in hanging pots. Keep moist in hot weather. Needs lots of light.
Thirstiness-med.

PLUMBAGO/Leadwort/jazmin azul

A climber but grows well as a shaped shrub. Pale/dark blue flower clusters early spring to late autumn. Prune to shape in late autumn after flowering has finished.
Thirstiness-med. Salt tolerant. Frost hardy.

PLUMERIA/Frangipani

Deciduous sub-tropical shrub/small tree. Flowers spring to late autumn. Creamy yellow, highly scented flowers.
Thirstiness-med. Perfumed.

POLYGALA DALMAISIANA/Sweet pea shrub

Tall shrub. Dark pink pea-like, flowers most of the year in mild climates.Trim lightly throughout the year to keeps its shape especially after flowering.
Thirstiness-med. Salt tolerant. Frost hardy.

PROTASPARAGUS/Asparagus Fern (Densiflorus)

Has bright green, fine, pin-like feathery leaves. Tiny fragrant flowers in summer followed by small berries. Yellowing foliage and leaf drop from too much sun and soil drying out. Susceptible to root rot if over-watered. Needs good light. Cut back to shape. **Thirstiness-med.**

PYRACANTHA ANGUSTIFOLIA/Orange firethorn

Shrub with glossy green leaves and very spiky branches. Small white flowers spring to summer. Winter, bright orange berries. Needs sun to keep bright berry colour. In a large pot keep trimmed to shape. Good on a large terrace. **Thirstiness-med. Salt tolerant. Frost hardy.**

ROSMARINUS PROSTRATUS/Trailing rosemary

Small, low-growing evergreen shrub with dark green, narrow, pencil-like scented leaves. Small blue flower spring to winter. Trim to shape when its gets leggy.
Thirstiness-low. Salt tolerant. Frost hardy.

RUSSELIA/Coral plant

Evergreen. Wiry, almost leafless stems with cascading tubular red/orange flowers. Flowers most of year in good conditions. Trim when it gets leggy
Thirstiness-med. Salt tolerant.

SALVIA LEUCANTHA/Velvet sage

Non-edible herb. Grey-green leaves bearing beautiful soft mauve/white, arching flowers in spring and autumn. Tall. New plants emerge from base of plant. Prune back spent flowering stems in late winter.
Thirstiness-med. Frost hardy.

SALVIA ELEGANS /Scarlet pineapple/Salvia rutilans

Edible herb. Tasty pineapple scented leaves and flowers for salads and infusions. Bright red flowers late summer and autumn. Prune lightly in late autumn and it may flower again in spring. New plants grow from base.
Thirstiness-med. Frost hardy.

SANSEVIERIA/Mother-in-law's tongue

Stiff, erect (agave-like) green and cream leaves. Allow soil to dry out between watering. Too much moisture causes rotting of the base and roots. This plant also does well in shade.
Thirstiness-low. Salt tolerant.

SCHEFFLERA ARBORICOLA/Hawaiian elf

Evergreen shrub with windmill-shaped green or variegated leaves. Keep pruned to shape.
Thirstiness-med.

STRELITZIA/Bird of paradise/Ave de paraíso

Clump-forming perennial. Large, dramatic, bird-like orange and blue flowers late autumn/winter and sometimes spring and summer. Do best when roots are crowded in a pot. Cut out dead flowers at base of stem
Thirstiness-med. Salt tolerant.

SYRINGA VULGARIS/Common lilac/Lila

Deciduous tree with fragrant pink flowers in summer. Prune to shape after flowering.
Thirstiness-med. Perfumed. **Frost hardy.**

TRADESCANTIA PALLIDA/Purple heart spiderwort

Straggly stems with purple leaves and small pink flowers in summer/autumn. Useful trailing plant. Cut back hard to keep shape. Other varieties with different-coloured foliage.
Thirstiness-low. Salt tolerant.

THUJA /Cedar/Tuya

Attractive evergreen tree – green or gold foliage. Dwarf varieties make excellent specimens for larger containers. Keep trimmed to shape.
Thirstiness-med. Salt tolerant. Frost hardy.

VERBENA/Verbena

Many varieties. Some upright and some trailing. Flowers red, pink and purple from spring to winter.

Thirstiness-med.

BULBOUS This selection will give year-round colour but each type of bulb generally for short periods. Cut back flower head as soon as flowers are finished and leaves when they have died back, this builds up strength for next year.

AGAPANTHUS/African Lily/Agapantus

Blue or white flowers on long straight stems. Flowers throughout the summer. In the autumn cut out dead stems and any dead leaves. Roots like to be crowded in pot. Needs more watering in spring and summer

Thirstiness-low/med. Frost hardy.

AMARYLLIS/Belladona Lily

Plant bulbs in late summer for winter flowers. Many exotic varieties with different colours. Umbels of flowers appear on long stems in winter. Cut out flower stem when it has died back and put pot in shaded place over summer and then back in sitiu in October and start watering again.

Thirstiness-med. Frost hardy.

BERGENIA SCHMIDTII/Bergenia.

Large, fleshy, green leaves. Long stems with clusters of bright pink flowers late winter to early spring.

Thirstiness-med.

FREESIA/Freesia/Fresia

Plant bulbs in the autumn. Flowers of many colours in spring. When they have finished flowering, remove from pot and store in dry place until the autumn. Water in spring and summer.

Thirstiness-med. Frost hardy. Perfumed.

HEMEROCALLIS/Day lily

Late spring flowering. Striking red, orange and many other flower colours. The flowers turn their heads towards the sun and last a day. Clump-forming. Like semi-shade.

Thirstiness-med. Frost hardy.

HYACINTHUS/Hyacinth/Jacinto

Plant bulbs (2 or 3 to a pot) in late summer or early winter for spring flowers. Flower colours pink, white, cream and blue. Second-year flowers are generally poor so treat them as annuals.
Thirstiness-med. Perfumed.

IRIS XIPHIUM/Dutch Iris/Spanish Iris/Lirio

Clump-forming. Dutch iris purple/blue and Spanish iris flowers white/yellow. Flower in spring. When they have died back, cut out old growth. Put in semi-shady spot in summer and water very little until you bring them out again in late autumn. **Thirstiness-low. Frost hardy.**

LILIUM ASIATIC/ Asiatic Lily/Lirio Asiatic

Many varieties. Spring and summer flowering. Large range of colours
Thirstiness-low. Some perfumed. **Frost hardy.**

MIRABILIS JALAPA/Flower of the night/San Diego de noche.

Grows easily from seed to form deep-rooted rhizomes, summer/autumn flowering. First-year's flowers are single colours of pink, yellow, red etc. In second year flower colours mix to form a kaleidoscope of colour. Flowers open at dusk and are highly perfumed.
Thirstiness-med. Perfumed.

NARCISSI/Daffodils/Narciso

Can create bright winter displays in pots and window boxes. Wide range of flower forms and colours. Best left in to multiply and clump.
Thirstiness-med. Perfumed. **Frost hardy.**

TULBAGHIA/Society garlic

Grows in clumps and produces pink/lilac and white flowers from spring through to late winter. Divide clumps for new plants.
Thirstiness-med. Frost hardy.

CLIMBERS – All best supported on trellises, walls or railings.

BOUGAINVILLA GLABRA/Glabra/Bouganvillea

Produces purple flowers nearly all the year in mild climates. Grows well as a standard. Prune well late winter to keep its shape. Susceptible to mealy bug if you over-water.

Thirstiness-med. Frost hardy.

CAMPIS GRANDIFLORA/(Bignonia family)/Chinese trumpet vine

Deciduous. Clings to walls with aerial roots. Beautiful red/orange trumpet flowers from early spring to late summer. Prune back to shape in winter

Thirstiness-med. Frost hardy.

JASMINUM OFFICINALE/Common jasmine/Jazmín de verano

Semi-evergreen. Clusters of white flowers spring to late summer. Trim lightly during flowering season and in late winter trim back hard to shape. Use the flowers for a refreshing infusion.

Thirstiness-med. Frost hardy.

JASMINUM POLYANTHUM/Pink jasmine

Pink and white flower buds open into highly perfumed white flowers in spring and summer. Trim back leggy off shoots when flowering has finished.

Thirstiness-med. Highly perfumed. **Salt tolerant. Frost hardy.**

MANDEVILLA (Dipladenia)/Mandevilla

Woody climbers. Glossy green leaves and trumpet-shaped flowers in red, pink, yellow or white summer through to winter.

Thirstiness-med.

PANDOREA JASMINOIDES (Bignonia family)/Bower vine

Shiny green leaves. Pale pink trumpet flowers with red centre from late spring to early autumn. Trim lightly in early winter

Thirstiness-med. Frost hardy.

PASSIFLORA/Passion flower/Flor de pasion

Semi-evergreen. Many different varieties some very exotic. Flowers early summer to late autumn. Trim back to shape in winter.

Thirstiness-med. Some varieties frost hardy.

ROSA/Rose/Rosal

Many varieties to chose from but ask for a perfumed variety. Cut back hard in winter to control size and stimulate new flowering growth.

Thirstiness-med. Perfumed. Frost hardy.

SOLANUM JASMINOIDES/Potato vine/Solanum trepador

Semi-evergreen. Has scented white flowers from spring to late autumn. Trim to keep tidy during summer and prune back to shape in winter

Thirstiness-med. Perfumed.

SOLANUM RANTONNETII/Blue potato bush

More shrub-like but grows well up trellis work. Violet/blue flowers late spring to autumn. Trim to keep tidy during summer and prune back to shape in winter. **Thirstiness-med.**

C. PLANTS THAT PREFER SEMI-SHADE.

AECHMEA (Bromeliad)/Aechmea/Achemia

Tropical but will tolerate some cold. Many different varieties with spectacular flowers. Allow soil to dry out before watering. Mist occasionally with rainwater in very hot weather. Water less in winter. New plants grow out from the base.

Thirstiness-med.

AZALIA (Rhododendron family) Azalia

Small, woody-stemmed shrub sold as pot plant. Small leaves, pink, red to white and mixed flowers autumn/winter. Acid-loving. Don't allow to dry out or get waterlogged. Water with rainwater. Use special feed for acid loving plants. Deadhead regularly.

Thirstiness-med. Frost hardy.

BEGONIA REX/Painted leaf begonia

Grown for leaf colours as well as flowers. To help humidity in hot weather stand on tray of pebbles with water. Do not mist spray them as may rot.

Thirstiness-med.

CAPSICUM ANNUM/Christmas pepper

Annuals grown for their coloured non-edible fruits to brighten up your terrace at Christmas. Never allow soil to dry out. Need good light but not direct sunlight.

Thirstiness-med.

CHLOROPHYTUM/Spider plant

Grown for their pale green and cream foliage. Propagate from new plantlets that grow on flowering stems.

Thirstiness-med.

CLIVIA/Kaffir lily

A bulb. Evergreen, with long, dark-green, strap-like leaves. Umbels of beautiful orange flowers on long, thick stems appear in winter.

Thirstiness-med.

CYCLAMEN/Cyclamen

Many different colours. Flower autumn to spring. Water from base of pot, never over the crown. When dying back in spring put in shady place, pot on its side and leave until new growth appears in late summer. Reposition pot and start watering again. Also pot up any dried seeds from previous year

Thirstiness-med. Frost hardy.

FICUS BENGAMINI/Weeping fig/Ficus Benjamin

Tropical evergreen tree. Oval shiny leaves. Keep leaves clean and mist with rainwater in very hot dry weather to stop leaf damage. Allow soil to dry out between watering. Don't like fluctuating temperatures or too much shade. Variegated varieties need plenty of light.

Thirstiness-med.

FICUS ELASTICA/Rubber plant

Tropical evergreen tree. Thick stem with large, thick, shiny, dark-green leaves, also variegated varieties. Keep leaves clean. Allow soil to dry out between watering.

Thirstiness-med. Salt tolerant.

FUCHSIA THALÍA/Fuchsia thalia/Fucsia thalia

A fuchsia that seems to survive better than most in hot climates. Dark velvety leaves with dark purple undersides. Long tubular orange/red flowers spring to late winter.
Thirstiness-med.

GARDENIA/Gardenia

Small evergreen shrub with highly scented white/cream flowers and dark glossy green leaves. Water well and mist spray in hotter months and feed regularly to promote flowers.
Thirstiness-med. Perfumed.

HEDERA SAGITTAEFOLIA/Needlepoint ivy

One of many varieties. Green-leafed and variegated. Mist leaves in hot weather to avoid browning of leaf tips. Never let soil dry out completely. Use as supported climbers or trailing from pots and window boxes.
Thirstiness-med. Salt resistant. Mainly frost hardy.

HYDRANGEA/Hydrangea/Hortensia

Deciduous shrubs. Like to be cool. Water with rain water and feed during flowering season – spring/summer with feed for acid-loving plants. Cut out dead flowers when they have dried out.
Thirstiness-high. Salt tolerant. Frost hardy.

IMPATIENS/Busy lizzie/Alegria

Annuals but in mild climates flower all year long. Darker-leaved varieties are hardier. Many different colours to brighten up terrace. Take cuttings by breaking off side shoot, leave in water until roots form. Put piece of charcoal in water to stop stem rotting. **Thirstiness-high. Salt tolerant.**

KALANCHOE BLOSSFELDIANA/Flaming Katy

Small, bushy, succulent-type plant. Many different colours. Do not over-water as stems will rot.
Thirstiness-med.

MONSTERA/Swiss cheese plant (Related to the Philodendron)

A climber with large, bright green, glossy leaves. Some grow well up moss poles. Brown patches on leaves and rotting roots caused by over-watering as well as being too cold in winter.
Thirstiness-med.

PERICALLIS/Cineraria

Daisy-like flowers in many multi colours. Tolerates poor compost and high temperatures. Doesn't like high humidity or being waterlogged. Shelter from heavy rain.

Thirstiness-med. Salt tolerant.

PLECTRANTUS AUSTRALIS/Money plant/Planta de dinero

Perennial. Green, trailing leaves with dainty, tubular, pale pink flowers. Cut out growing tips to keep plant busy. Good in hanging pots.

Thirstiness-med.

PRIMULA/Polyanthus

Mostly grown as annuals. Flower autumn to spring. Many different bright colours.

Thirstiness-med. Perfumed. Frost hardy.

SCHLUMBERGERA TRUNCATA/Christmas cacti/Cactus de Navidad

Flowers in winter. Many different colours. To water put pebbles and water in base tray. When flowering is over, put in shady dry place water infrequently. When new buds form in autumn, start watering regularly and give them more light once flowering.

Thirstiness-med.

STEPHANOTIS/Stephanotis

Evergreen climber with dark green shiny leaves. Clusters of fragrant white tubular flowers in spring. Grow well on trellis work on on hoops. Tie in new shoots and trim off excess to keep compact. Keep leaves clean. Very susceptible to mealy bug.

Thirstiness-med. Perfumed.

NOTE: You will note that Section D (on the right) includes no flowering plants and that all are evergreens with dark green leaves. Some plants that thrive in semi-shade can be moved into a shady situation during the summer or winter but for no longer than a couple of months.

D. PLANTS THAT PREFER SEMI-SHADE BUT CAN DO WELL IN SHADE WITH A REASONABLE AMOUNT OF REFLECTED LIGHT.

ALOE VERA/Medicinal aloe

Thick succulent leaves grow upwards. In spring when the plant is mature yellow flowers appear on long stems. The gel from the centre of the leaves used in treating burns, just one of many uses.

Thirstiness-low.

ASPIDISTRA/Cast iron plant/Hoja de salon

Dark-green, wide-arching leaves on stiff upright stems. Don't over-water or over-fertilise. Hot dry air can cause leaves to go brown at tips. Keep leaves clean. Mist in hot weather. Variegated varieties need better light.

Thirstiness-low.

CHAMAEDOREA ELEGANS/Parlour palm/Chamadorea

A pretty, single-stemmed feathery palm. Normally an indoor plant but good at the back of a sheltered, shaded terrace. Tolerates some neglect.

Thirstiness-med.

CISSUS RHOMBIFOLIA/Grape Ivy

Dark-green, medium-sized trailing leaves. Needs support to climb. Good trailing down from hanging pots. Keep moist and mist spray in hot weather. Keep leaves clean. Many other ivies to choose from.

Thirstiness-med.

HOWEA FORSTERIANA/Kentia palm

Graceful arching fronds that tolerate low light. Don't allow roots to dry out. Keep leaves clean.

Thirstiness-med. Salt tolerant.

NEPHROLEPIS CORDIFOLIA/Fishbone fern/Helecho

Tropical fern. One of the hardiest ferns. Many other ferns to choose for shady places.

Thirstiness-med.

E. NORTHERN EUROPEAN INDOOR PLANTS THAT CAN ADAPT TO MEDITERRANEAN CLIMATE SITUATIONS IF SPECIAL CARE IS TAKEN.

All need semi-shade with good, indirect light and completely sheltered from winds. Cut back watering in cooler weather. Mist spray to cool leaves in summer months.

AESCHYNANTHUS/ Lipstick vine/Columea

Fleshy, dark-green leaves with long, trailing stems. Red tubular flowers in summer. Feed during flowering season. Don't like fluctuating temperatures or draughts – cause leaves to drop.

Thirstiness-med.

CALATHEA/Peacock plant

Tropical evergreen. Dark-green leaves with many unusual patterns. Stand in shallow trays with pebbles and water and mist regularly in hot weather. Don't allow to dry out. Draughts cause leaf curl.

Thirstiness-med.

CORDYLINE FRUTICOSA/Ti plant/Dracena

Tropical. Long stems with attractive red/green leaves. Keep leaves clean. Allow surface soil to dry out between watering. Need high humidity so put with other like-minded plants and mist in hot weather.

Thirstiness-med.

DIEFFENBACHIA/Dumb cane/Diffenbacchia

Evergreen perennial. Dark-green leaves blotched with cream. Allow surface soil to dry out between watering to avoid rotting stems. Bugs – if too dry aphids, scale and red spider mite.

Thirstiness-med.

DRACAENA/Dracaena/Dracena

Tropical. Very striking leaves in various colours. Allow surface soil to dry out between watering. If they become bare at the base cut out top to encourage new growth.

Thirstiness-med.

EPIPREMNUM PINNATUM/Devil's Ivy/Pothos/Potos Aureum
Evergreen sub-tropical. Heart-shaped leaves with yellow blotches. With its thin, sticky, aerial roots can cling to terrace walls. Good in tall pots trailing down or hanging pots. Allow surface soil to dry out between watering.
Thirstiness-med.

NEPENTHES/Pitcher plant./Vaso de Venus
Also named fly-catcher plants because of the pendulous pitchers which attract and trap unsuspecting flies in the liquid, absorbing them as food. Grow in hanging pots. In colder areas bring inside in winter.
Thirstiness-med.

SPATHIPHYLLUM/Peace Lily
Attractive, green, lance-shaped leaves. They need enough light to produce their white, waxy, sail-shaped flowers from spring to autumn. Feed during flowering season.
Thirstiness-med.

PLANTS SUITABLE FOR HANGING BASKETS AND POTS.
Hanging baskets do not retain water as well as containers and window boxes. The number of plants suitable for them in hot climate conditions is therefore restricted. We suggest you try the following:

Begonia Rex
Chlorophytum
Crassula Multicava
Epicactus
Lantana Montevidensis
Petunia Sufina
Plectranthus Australis
Portulacaria Afra Variegata
Portulacas
Romero Prostatus
Schlum Bergera Truncata
Sedum Morganianum
Sedum Rubrotinctum
Tradescantia

4.3 Selecting the Best for Each Situation

There are several things to consider.

a. The direction your terrace balcony or windowsill faces. In general more varieties of plants can be grown successfully on east and west-facing terraces than south or north.

b. Whether you have awnings or blinds that can be used to protect your plants from the hottest hours of summer and winter suns, and the hottest summer and coldest winter gales. Compared to plants in a garden, plants in containers have a limited amount of compost to preserve a reserve of moisture. Also the thickness of container walls and the amount of compost, which prevent roots from cooking or freezing depending on their location, are limited.

c. Your exposure to natural winds and rain, unnatural winds and gusty, swirling rain funnelled between buildings and, in some more northerly and inland situations, wind-blown sleet or snow. If in such harsh situations look out for frost-resistant plants.

d. Your exposure to 'dirty' rain carrying red dust from north Africa that can coat everything including plants – some of which can be difficult to clean.

e. Your geographic location. Whether you are located in a sub-tropical, Mediterranean or temperate climate for much of the year. If sub-tropical then cacti and succulents will be sensible buys.

f. Your height in a tall building. Up-draughts can tear and burn delicate plants on the upper floors. The highest apartment with a balcony and small terrace in Benidorm is 43 floors up although glazed-in apartments go up to 52 floors.

Such phenomena are looked at in various sections of the book.

4.4. Making Seasonal Changes

Many of the plants described in the previous section flower for months each year for many years as they are perennial plants. Plants, shrubs and trees with root systems can survive in containers for some years without becoming totally root-bound and their life expectancy can be lengthened by re-potting before this occurs.

However, some of the plants have only a short flowering period and in some cases short lives. For instance annuals and perennial bulbs and poinsettias. The latter being by nature long-living perennials which are especially force-grown in hothouses for short end of year displays.

You may therefore wish to include seasonal changes in your annual planting plan and plant budget. For instance you could choose the following sequences in window boxes, groups of pots or larger containers. Each sequence will give you good all-year-round colour without any plant becoming boring.

SEQUENCE 1:   Spring and to mid-summer – petunias
Mid-summer to mid-autumn – portulacas
Mid-autumn to end of early spring – pansies or violas

SEQUENCE 2:   Spring/ summer – busy lizzies
Autumn/winter – ageratum

SEQUENCE 3:   Spring – irises
Summer – lilies
Autumn – cyclamens
Winter – freesias

SEQUENCE 4:   Spring – messems
Summer/autumn – vincas
Christmas – poinsettias
Winter – chrysanthemums

SEQUENCE 5:   Spring/summer – begonia
Autumn/winter – decorative brassicas

To help you develop other sequences the typical flowering times of plants are included in the plant descriptions of Section 4.2.

4.5 Effective Colour Combinations

In our earlier book *Your Garden in Spain* we included a chapter titled 'Painting with plants' for when living in Spain one has an amazing range of native and imported plants with flowers and leaves in every colour, tint and hue of the rainbow.

Although the number of plants suitable for your terrace is less than if you had a sizeable garden, the range of colours is still there for you chose from. So in this section we outline the possibilities for everyone – even with little eye for colour – to create plant displays that are attractive and perhaps stunning when seen through balcony doorways, when sitting out or working on the terrace, from community gardens or adjacent streets and the beach in the case of frontline apartments. Those apartment-owners that have plant arranging, painting or interior design skills can have a field day.

The start point is to recognise that the colours of individual flowers, groups of mixed flowers plus the very many colours of leaves offer endless possibilities for both sedate and exciting displays. Simple and creative displays that produce just the right effect for each windowsill, balcony/terrace railing, balustrade wall, corner and wall space from floor to ceiling. And don't forget the cool impact of an area of white flowers. White is the world's

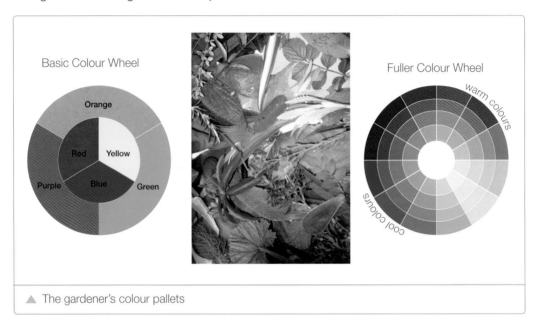

Basic Colour Wheel

Orange

Red   Yellow

Purple   Blue   Green

Fuller Colour Wheel

warm colours

cool colours

▲ The gardener's colour pallets

prime colour which separates into the other colours when light is split by water droplets to create rainbows and when passed through diamonds, cut glass and ice crystals.
The possibilities are illustrated by the following seven types of window box display each according to our Seven Cs of colour combining. The same ideas apply to individual or groups of plants whether in pots, containers, wall pouches etc. Recognise that you can create each of the effects with flowers and leaf colours together or separately and that some plants also offer interesting trunk and branch colours.

The choices are yours. The following are intended as thought-starters. Nothing is right or wrong. After all it is your apartment. Consider some bold daring colour schemes as well as more subdued traditional ones.

Possibly consider different colour schemes for seasonal plant changes including cool ones for the summer and warmer ones for the winter. Use your past experiences, what you remember seeing when travelling, and use your imagination. And you have another possibility up your sleeve that is not available in a garden. If allowed by the community or local authority regulations, you can paint the walls of your terraces to create a variety of backgrounds for your plants although in most cases white has the best Mediterranean effect.

THE SEVEN Cs OF COLOUR COMBINING

1. COMMON COLOURS

Plant up with a single type or mix of plants with a single flower colour or a common foliage colour if going for evergreen foliage plants.

e.g. Window box: summer-blue petunias; winter-bright yellow pansies. Container: bougainvillea, hydrangea, oleander or heather.

2. COMPATIBLE COLOURS

Plant up with plants of one or several types which have flowers and/or foliage in closely matching harmonious shades or hues of a selected colour.

e.g. Window box: summer – petunias, busy lizzies, portulacas; winter – cyclamen in various shades of pink, ornamental cabbages, campanula/ petunia. Container: Verbena, bamboo, tradescanthia.

3. COMPLEMENTARY COLOURS

Co-planting several plants of the same or different types that have vividly different colours but which go well with each other.

e.g. Window box: summer – geraniums, petunias; winter – chrysanthemums, pansies. Container: Euryops with messems in front, dipladenias.

4. CLASHING COLOURS

Purposely planting together a group of plants with very different bright colours which clash to make a very bold statement.

e.g. Window box: summer – portulacas, petunias; winter – cyclamens, portulacas, pansies. Container: Mix of hibiscus or a mix of leonothis/red geraniums/ purple bougainvillea/ orange begonias.

5. CALMING COLOURS

Purposely planting together plants whose flower and foliage colours create no clashes but rather a sense of restful harmony between flowers and foliages or foliages.

e.g. Window box: all-year-round – grey cacti, lavenders and light blue petunias, mix of cordylines. Container: lavenders with blue agapanthus and society garlic, herb collection, grey cacti.

6. COLD / COOL COLOURS

An extension of '5' using only a mix of cold-looking white and mauve flowers and grey leaves that look cool even at midday on a mid-summer day.

e.g. Window box: summer – white petunias with trailing white lantanas; winter – white cyclamens, pansies, azaleas or chrysanthemums. Container: white petunias and begonias, white and blue plumbago and solanum potato vine.

7. CALIENTE (HOT) COLOURS

Purposely planting a single red plant or a mix of the most vivid reds, oranges and yellows you can find to create a balcony or terrace hot spot.

e.g.Window box: summer – bright red geraniums, red carnations, bromeliads; winter: poinsettias and croton, kalenchoas, red azaleas, Christmas peppers. Container: bottle brush, leonothis, pineapple sage, French marigolds, cockscomb, red geraniums

In practice you can use the plant photographs included in Section 4.2 to help develop several possibilities before you go to the garden centre to buy your plants.

When you arrive at the garden centre place some of the selected plants in a window box, pot or other container to assess what the effect will be in practice. If in doubt try out a few more possibilities before making the final purchase. And don't forget that interesting long-life combinations of evergreen plants can be planted.

Most garden centres will be quite happy for you to make up trial window boxes and other containers. After all you are the customer and if you are happy with your buys you will be back in the future.

As you see, that is what we did for the photographs above. You might even give them some ideas for their own displays. Some garden centres will go further and plant up containers for you.

We used window boxes for the illustrative photographs above in order to produce a common format that fitted neatly into the text. Obviously colour combining applies to the planting of every type of container as illustrated below.

4.6 Natural Aromatherapy and Air Improvement

A. PERFUME

If you select and plant a few perfumed plants, you will add another dimension to your terraces. For example, a subtle background aroma throughout the day from aromatic herbs, at dusk the deep perfume of a lady of the night (Galán de noche) pumped out in bursts from the small trumpet-like flowers, or the perfume of jasmine or an exotic, perfumed climbing rose such as Belle Portuguese or The Generous Gardener on either side of a balcony doorway.

We indicate which plants emit a noticeable perfume in the plant descriptions of Section 4.2.

Of those included in the plant descriptions our favourite 10 perfumed plants for balconies and terraces are as follows:

1. Amaryllis, Beladonna lily
2. Cestrum nocturnum, Lady of the night
3. Freesia, Freesia
4. Geranium graveolens, Scented geranium
5. Jasminum polyanthum, Pink jasmine
6. Lilium Asiatic, Asiatic lily
7. Lavendula dentate, French lavender
8. Mirabilis jalapa, Flower of the night
9. Rosa, Climbing rose
10. Solanum, Potato vine

B. POLLUTION

Recently there have been claims that plants can help reduce air pollution in homes and offices. It therefore makes sense to include some of the most effective plants on your terraces, balconies and windowsills. These include the following:

- For absorbing electromagnetic radiation – eg., cacti, spider plant, spathiphyllum.
- Chemical/exhaust pollutions – ficus bengamini, bamboo, ivy, geraniums, asparagus fern, pine and oak trees.
- Disinfecting the air/anti-bacterial – lemon, geranium, amaryllis, agapanthus, garlic.

By chance all these are in our selection of plants except oak and pine trees, which can be included in collections of native plants mentioned on page 102.

4.7 Minimum Maintenance Plants

One of the reasons you purchased an apartment rather than a villa with a garden is that you did not want the work involved in laying out, planting and maintaining a large garden under the hot Mediterranean sun. Perhaps because you are retired or infirm, or know nothing about plants. It therefore makes sense to select plants for windowsills, balconies and terraces that don't need too much work. Unless, of course, you are a frustrated gardener for whom gardening is your life line and, being constrained by the restricted space, you want to spend as many hours of the day as possible developing a botanical garden.

In making the selection of plants listed in Section 4.2 we chose those especially suitable for small spaces and deliberately left out large plants, shrubs and trees that require extensive pruning. But some of those included will need occasional pruning to maintain a pleasing size and shape and many flowering plants will benefit from deadheading to stimulate continuous or repeat flowerings. The latter will be discussed more fully in Section 5.8. Unfortunately a few of the plants we list do have a regular leaf fall that needs tidying up but the visual impact of the plant offsets this chore.

Many annuals will only flower continuously if every few days you remove dying flowers before they create seed pods. We therefore minimised the number of plants that easily go to seed and maximised the number of long-flowering plants plus a few plants whose flowers are sparse but spectacular, plants that rarely flower but are worth waiting for and some evergreen non-flowering plants.

The more drought-resistant and slow-growing plants you use the less watering and feeding you will need to do and this will also reduce the incidences of fungal and insect attacks, which are mostly brought on by damp and humid conditions and an abundance of weak unnaturally fast growth. If you do have thirsty plants, mini irrigation systems are available these days.

If you allow plants to spread so that it becomes difficult to see the surface of the compost, you should rarely be bothered with weeds. Any unwanted seeds that germinate with be smothered or die because they have been starved of essential sunlight.

When planting a rockery or cacti bed on a large open terrace, plant through black plastic mulched with stone or lava chippings or holes in a preformed plastic landscape to minimise the possibility of weeds.

Naturally, if you plant fruit trees in containers, they will need twice a year pruning (see Part Eight) and, if you decide to grow vegetables in containers, window boxes or growing tables, this will require more work than a collection of drought-resistant, slow-growing succulents or cacti. However, if you decide to do these two things, you will have already decided that the time required – relatively little once you are set up – is well worth it for the healthy, fresh, ecologically grown, seasonal produce you will be able to harvest at any time of day even while enjoying your evening sundowner.

We have actually seen a real lawn on a rooftop but we don't recommend that you try to replicate this. But if you love the feel and look of grass there are some very acceptable artificial turf products available these days which can be occasionally vacuum-cleaned. There will not be the need for the daily sweep of a dusty terrace.

4.8 Possibilities for Developing Plant Collections

If you are living in an apartment, you may well have more time on your hands than if you live in a villa so it may be of interest to develop a collection of the different varieties of a specific group of plants. This can be both fascinating and beneficially time-consuming especially if often alone or living alone.

Among the best groups of plants for developing collections are succulents and cacti on any aspect-facing terraces and for experienced or courageous new gardeners-bulbs, bonsais or orchids.

Typically the best locations for some popular collections are as follows:

Type of plants	Covered terrace facing:				Open terrace or rooftop	In south-facing or winter-heated glazed
	South	East	West	North		
Succulents	★	★	★	★	★	★
Cacti	★	★		★	★	★
Bonsais			★			
Cyclamens		★	★	★		
Herbs	★	★	★	★	★	
Geraniums	★	★	★	★	★	★
Bulbs		★	★	★		
Wild plants		★	★	★	★	

Collections can be built up by keeping one's eyes open at garden centres, florists, garden club plant stalls, market stalls, *rastro* stalls; by joining a specialist plant group such as a bonsai or rare bulb group such as www.heritagbulbs.com; by obtaining cuttings or already rooted young plants from friends; by growing from seed as outlined in Section 4.9.

A collection of wild plants grown from seeds or seedlings or trees grown from saplings can be interesting to those interested in the Mediterranean autochthonous fauna. Seeds can be obtained from www.semillassilvestres.com and plants from building sites or roadsides. A mini biosphere would be possible.

4.9. Growing New Plants From Cuttings

It is relatively easy to produce – propagate – new plants from cuttings of some of your favourite plants or from a friend's plants that you are especially attracted by, but not all.

Propagating is especially useful if you are wishing to develop a more prominent display of a particular plant, add a special plant to your existing mix of plants or build up a collection. The several ways of propagating new plants and typical plants for each method are illustrated below.

ROOT CUTTINGS

Typical plants: Many herbs and perennials.
Method: Pull or dig out a stem with roots from outside of plant or remove plant from container and cut into several plants. Plant into nursery or final container.
When best to do: spring and autumn.

STEM CUTTINGS

Typical plants: Geraniums, busy lizzies, fuschias, pothos, europs.
Method: Cut off a strong stem at a leaf node. Cut into 15 to 25cm lengths with a leaf node at the top and bottom. Remove all leaves except for two to five at the top. Push cutting into compost in a nursery pot.
When best to do: spring and autumn.

SIDE SHOOT CUTTINGS

Typical plants: Euryops, chrysanthemums, margaritas, geraniums.
Method: Gently pull off a strong side-shoot complete with a centimetre-long heel. Plant up as for stem cuttings.
When best to do: spring and summer.

LEAF CUTTINGS

Typical plants: Succulents, cacti, cyclamens, bignonias campsis.
Method: Pull or cut of a leaf and bury stem or cut end in compost in a nursery pot. A new plant will start to grow within a few weeks.
When best to do: Spring and summer.

AERIAL OFFSPRINGS

Typical plants: Spider plant (1), some kalanchoes (2) and epicactus (3).
Method: Cut off small offspring plants hanging on a long stem from main plant (1), forming on edge of leaves (2) or a branch with air roots at its base (3) and pot up in compost.
When best to do: Any time of year.

Cuttings can root more quickly if they are planted in a mini greenhouse made from a 5 or 7-litre plastic water bottle or in a pot covered with a sealed plastic bag. Only have the compost just damp and spray surface with a natural fungicide such as propolis before planting cuttings.

4.10 Growing Something Special from Seeds

We have included 140 useful plants/plant groups for apartment terraces, balconies and window sills in Section 4.2. As said earlier, these were chosen on the basis of ease of maintenance, survival in coastal and inland situations and to give you a good range of plant sizes and colours to choose from. Naturally there are others that an experienced gardener might like to try especially if they previously grew plants from seeds. Some plants are relatively easy to raise from seed to seedlings and then to mature plants. Others are decidedly a challenge even for the expert.

For example: easy seeds for beginners include avocado, nasturtiums, petunias, marigolds, sunflowers, and vincas.

Moderately easy seeds worth a try with a little experience include geraniums, cacti and passion flowers.

Decidedly difficult seeds, which some dedicated, experienced gardeners confined to apartment terraces will undoubtedly go for because they like the challenge of producing something rare and beautiful, include bulbs, mango, some cacti and mini bananas.

Some of the easiest seeds are now available in inexpensive kits that include a growing tray, mini greenhouse cover, compost and seeds.

English language catalogues that offer the largest number of flowering and evergreen plant and tree seeds include:

For popular well-known varieties with a few new introductions each year – www.thompson-morgan.com, www.suttons-seeds.co.uk

For a wide range of interesting, often rare, unusual and exotic seeds – www.chilternseeds.co.uk, www.jungleseeds.co.uk

For Spanish wild plants – www.semillassilvestres.com

The following is a basic guide for growing plants from seeds. A more detailed guide will be found in Section 6.13 in our earlier sister book *Your Garden in Spain – From planning to planting and maintenance.*

1. Select and buy your seeds. Check the date stamp on the packet as seeds more than one or two years old can be difficult to germinate. Indeed in some cases best success will come from growing your own very fresh seeds.

2. Prepare your compost mix. For small seeds we suggest you use only vermiculite and for large seeds a commercial or home-made seed compost (see 8 below).

3. Read the instructions on the packet or sent with the seeds. A few seeds will require special treatments like soaking in water for 24 hours or going in the refrigerator for a month.

4. Fill your trays or pots with compost. Firm with a piece of wood or bottom of empty water bottle.

5. Sow seeds. Small seeds just on the surface and covered with a sprinkling of vermiculite. Larger seeds pushed into holes made in the compost with the end of a pencil.

6. Dampen compost with a mist sprayer with water which includes a few drops of

propolis or another ecological fungicide to stop seedlings rotting off..

7. Place pot or tray under a transparent propagator cover or in a heated propagator. Then place in a light semi shaded warm place. If you place on a window sill in the sun as you did in northern Europe there is a good chance of seeds drying up as soon as they germinate.

8. When the seeds have germinated and produced seedlings with two to four small leaves, prick them out into individual small pots, larger pots for several seedlings or a tray with space for many. In general leave four centimetres between seedlings or use cellular polystyrene trays. Use a proprietary seed compost or home-produced mix of three parts plant compost, one part sand and one part vermiculite.

9. Sprinkle a few granules of an ecological snail/slug killer on the surface of the compost.

10. Keep the compost just damp and after a month start to feed young plants with a few drops of a flowering plant liquid fertiliser in water.

11. Gradually move the young plants into a situation that receives sun for a few hours a day.

12. Plant plants when large and strong enough into the final containers in a potting compost.

4.11 Native Trees

As mentioned in section 4.8, interesting collections of indigenous or native trees can be developed on apartment terraces. The trees can be grown as sizeable specimens in pots or as bonsais in trays as illustrated. Bonsais need a sun blind and daily watering in the summer. The trees can be grown by collecting self-seeded saplings or fallen seeds. Seeds and small trees can also be obtained from Spain's two specialist suppliers – www.semillassilvestres.com for seeds and www.cultidelta.com for trees.

4.12 Creative Use of Dried Flowers

▲ Typical dried flowers

One tends to think of live flowers, but if one had a garden in a Mediterranean climate situation, it would be relatively easy to grow several varieties of dried flowers for summer harvesting and drying in bunches. However, except on large open terraces and penthouse and town house roofs, it is not the best use of space to grow them from seed because dried bunches are often sold in flower shops, herb stalls in markets, herbal shops and at meetings of flower-arranging clubs and groups.

If you do decide to grow them from seed, the best to grow on terraces are helidryson and limonium.

Bunches can be displayed in vases, in bunches hanging individually in corners of the ceiling or as a display hanging from a circular hoop or cane or metal rod hung from the ceiling.

Bunches hung in the corners of the ceiling as well as looking attractive may well attract geckoes which are wonderful to watch after dark as they stalk a variety of flying insects for dinner.

4.12 Artificial Flowers and Plants Can Be Useful

Don't throw your hands up in horror. Some people are just not green-fingered or have absolutely no time to care for plants but would still like a pretty flowery or planty feel to their terrace. There are now some attractive well-designed and manufactured artificial flowers, flowering branches, flowering and evergreen plants and even small trees and cacti plants available if one hunts around. Good sources can include home-furnishing shops, flower shops, Chinese emporiums, garden centres, tutors to flower arranging clubs and stalls at meetings, container shops and even market stalls. Although silk and textile flowers often look the most real, plastic ones will last longer where they can get wet when it rains. The possibilities for their use include:

- Displays in weighted vases on sideboards, tables and storage cupboards. If not weighted vases will be soon knocked over and broken. The easiest thing is to fill vases with sand.

▲ Typical artificial flowers and plants

- Displays in window boxes or pots on high up, difficult-to-see windowsills to just give a hint of colour.

- A floor-placed window box or pots in shady places where few flowering plants will survive.

- Climbing up trellis work.

- Individual bunches hanging in bunches in ceiling corners or as arrow of bunches tied to hanging rails or an antique metal circular hanger used for drying and storing sausage products.

- Bushes and trees used to create internal divisions on large terraces or to fill corner displays.

The benefits are that they can last for years with no care and maintenance except for an occasional cleaning.

But there are some potential problems.

▲ Artificial poinsettias

a. Their colours can fade if exposed to direct sunlight or strong reflected sunlight.

b. They can fall apart or decay if allowed to become wet from driving rain.

c. They can become dusty if not washed shaken or vacuum cleaned several times a year.

d. Even an attractive display can become boring in time so you might want to have seasonal displays. Even we were fooled by these plastic poinsettias when we took the photograph. The display was perfect after a month and could be washed and put away until next December.

e. Cheap products look cheap. Ones that look more real than real are normally expensive. The best can be very expensive.

Buying and caring for your plants

Provides practical guidelines and skills for buying and caring for your terrace, balcony and windowsill plants throughout the year.

5.1 Sources of Plants

Once you have decided on the type of colour scheme and types of plants to use, the next thing is to go out and find your plants. Naturally your nearest garden centre is the obvious first port of call, especially if you are only looking for some of the most popular plants for a group of pots or window box or two. But it is still worth looking round at a number of other garden centres, especially those which still grow some of their own plants rather than buying in all of their plants from Spanish, European or international growers (as is the case more and more). This can result in significant variations in quality and prices. If you are looking beyond a few basic plants, there are other sources of plants worth investigating. Some will make for an interesting outing. Once you find reliable competitively priced garden centres etc. stick with them and make friends with the staff. They can be very helpful and supportive for regular customers.

12 POPULAR SOURCES OF PLANTS

1. Nurseries that grow most of the plants they sell. Often located inland. Plants are normally hardened off before sale and grown in good, sometimes self-formulated, compost mixes.

2. Garden centres that buy in most or even all of the plants they sell. Many may be imported and grown under ideal forced conditions in heated greenhouses and are not fully hardened off before sale. There is sometimes a problem in integrating the compost in which the plants were purchased with the compost you buy to place in your containers when one type dries out faster than the other.

3. Flower shops that often only sell a small range of plants. But recognise that they can sit in the shop or on the pavement outside for some time.

4. Weekly markets that have stalls selling imported or own grown plants. Often a good turnover of plants but can be damaged during bad weather.

5. Gardening club plant stalls where enthusiastic amateurs sell their own propagated plants to members and visitors to raise club funds. Normally well-raised plants in good compost mixes.

6. Growing circles – see Section 1.10 where one or two members might focus on growing flowering plants and vegetable plantlets for bartering with other members.

7. Local agricultural cooperatives – tend to be best for vegetable plantlets and fruiting trees. Often a source of bulbs.

8. Swaps of plants or cuttings with friends.

9. Neighbours about to move elsewhere within the Med or back home to more northerly climes.

10. Your own growing of plants from cuttings or seeds. The quality of plants is entirely in your hands! The best seeds are often those which you collect from some of your own plants for drying and storing to sow next spring.

11. Mail order plant and seed catalogues willing to export to the Mediterranean countries.

12. Plastic plants from markets, pot shops and Chinese emporiums.

5.2 Tips for Buying Your Plants

First: buy your plants at the most appropriate time of year. For instance, don't buy summer annuals or delicate plants before any chance of air frosts is past . Also don't buy summer annuals after midsummer when they will be more difficult to establish than in the spring. Last and most important: ensure that you select plants that have:

a. No sign of disease or infestations.

b. A good-sized pot which contain the roots in relation to the size of the growth above the ground. A safe plant will have foliage no more than one-and-a-half times the width of the pot. One with foliage three times the width of the pot will be very risky.

c. A good shape with strong junctions between the branches and the trunk.

d. Just one or two open flowers so that you can be sure of the colour and plenty of forming new buds. Plants purchased in full flower with little sign of follow-on buds will soon finish flowering as the plants' priority when first planted in containers will be to put down roots. Yes, many garden centres do market plants in full flower, but some now charge more for budded but unflowered plants than those in full flower.

e. No sign of supportive canes and ties chaffing or cutting into the bark.

f. No sign of wind or frost burn if buying in the winter or early spring .

g. No sign of being stressed by heat or being allowed to dry out.

h. No sign of having been waterlogged or fungal attacks where the stem emerges from the compost.

If the garden centre does not have the variety or colour of flower you want, ask if they can order it for you. If not, try somewhere else.

Prices in one garden centre can be twice those of another so if the plants you are looking for seem overly expensive check out other garden centres and market stalls.

Once your terrace balcony and windowsills are planted up ensure that the expensive, unplanned, impromptu purchase of a special/unusual plant that catches your eye can be fitted in by moving pots around or replacing an existing plant before parting with your money. If you have a large terrace and plan to have large shrubs and trees such as palms and olive trees, check that the garden centre can deliver for you at a reasonable cost. Remember crane hire is expensive so buy no larger than will fit into the lift and let the shrubs and trees grow to your planned size on the terrace.

5.3 Understand the Nano Climate that Your Plants Require

Three aspects of climate will influence the relative success and failures you will have in growing your plants.

Firstly, the macro climate of your geographic area – which includes the general pattern of annual and seasonal hours of sunshine, temperatures, winds, humidity, rain, and frost hail and snow. This will determine the most suitable flowering and evergreen plants, herbs, fruit trees and vegetables for your area.

Secondly, the micro climate of your terraces, balconies and window boxes – which includes very localised temperatures which can be affected by direct and reflected sunshine, the cool and hot air blown out from the airconditioning, exposure to winds, shade from a tree or blind, heat loss around windows and doors and through the glass.

Thirdly, the nano climate surrounding each individual plant – this is the very localised conditions above and below ground affecting the foliage and roots of each and every individual plant.

The diagram below illustrates the characteristics of bad and good nano climates. A good

Characteristics of: POOR NANO CLIMATE	GOOD NANO CLIMATE
ABOVE GROUND 1. Compost surface baked hard and dirty with dead leaves etc.. 2. Watering of leaves and flowers. 3. Constant chemical insecticide/fungicide mist. 4. All insects even if beneficial killed off. 5. Exposure to worst of hottest suns and coldest winds.	**ABOVE GROUND** 1. Compost surface kept loose and clean of dead leaves etc. 2. Surface watering, unless via roots. 3. Only eco sprays and water leaf misting. 4. Beneficial insects allowed to live. 5. Shading/shelter from hottest sun and coldest winds.
BELOW GROUND 1. Compost lacks any natural nutrients. 2. Compost a hard, compacted, solid lump. 3. Sterile compost, hardly a microbe and no worms. 4. Widely varying moisture. Either dried out or waterlogged. 5. Roots constrained and constantly fed with fast-acting chemical fertilisers.	**BELOW GROUND** 1. Natural nutrients available in the compost. 2. Open, crumbly, aerated compost structure. 3. Full of beneficial unseen microbes, and even some worms. 4. Constant moisture, never waterlogged. 5. Roots able to spread and find and what they need from the compost.

nano climate is critical to plants in containers and easily improved by yourself.

Bear this in mind from the day you plant up your plants to the day you replace them.

5.4 Planting Up Your Plants

The planting up of your plants is the most important thing you will ever do for them. The following things are important.

SIZE OF CONTAINER

Plant individual plants in a pot twice the diameter of the foliage of the plant and twice to three times the depth of the pot the plant was purchased in. Give groups of plants to be planted in larger containers a similar space. Recognise that some plants such as strelitzia will perform better when several plants are planted close together in one container.

QUALITY COMPOST

Absolutely fundamental. It needs to retain moisture, allow excess water to drain away and will provide plants with nutrients. If possible buy a peat based compost that is pre-fertilized and preferable with other added organic materials and five percent of grit or sand. If not, add them in. Recognise that some crushed palm fibre composts tend to dry out too quickly. When planting cacti and succulents ensure that the compost is very free-draining. A sandy, unfertilized compost without an added weed killer sold as a spring top up for lawns is ideal. All composts can be improved by adding half a teaspoon to a teaspoonful of TerraCottem soil improver to each litre of compost used. This helps aerate, enrich and improve water holding needs of composts. Often watering can be reduced by 50 per cent.

DAMP COMPOST

The compost should be damp in the sack. If dried out, dampen in a bucket before using.

ACIDIC COMPOST

Purchase acidic compost for acid-loving plants such as azaleas, camellias, hydrangeas and heathers. Normally the sacks are clearly marked. You can raise the acidy level by dampening the compost with a dilute solution of cider vinegar in water.

FILLING CONTAINERS

Fill your selected container, firming as you go, until the container is full to within a centimetre of the top in small pots, two centimetres in medium sizes and four or five in large containers. This will prevent spillage when watering .

HOLE DEPTH AND WIDTH

Dig out a hole in the compost with a trowel the size of the soil in the pot housing the purchased plant. For convenience place the compost removed in an empty pot ready to use to fill in and firm around the plant.

REMOVAL OF PLANTS FROM POTS

Dampen the soil in the pot containing the plant. Then tap the pot and lift out the plant carefully avoiding knocking off lumps of compost. You may find it easier to do this with the pot held at 45 degrees to the vertical. If there is no sign of compacted roots around the circumference of the compost, plant immediately. If there are numerous roots bound together and going around the circumference of the compost ball, loosen them carefully before planting.

PLACING IN HOLE AND INFILLING

Carefully place the root ball in the dug hole and firm compost around the root ball. Add extra compost to fill the container up to the level of the compost attached to the plant being planted. If you have noticed slugs or snails around the terrace shake a few granules of an ecological bait. We use an ecological product such as Neudorff's 'Ferramol antilimicos'.

FIRST WATERING

Then give the compost around the roots a light watering to help the two types of compost integrate and prevent the compost around the root ball drying out and leaving an air gap.

SUPPORT IF NECESSARY

If a tall unsteady plant or a climber, provide a plastic or cane support or fix to a trellis, wall or railing.

HARDENING OFF

If you buy plants from a heated greenhouse especially in early spring or late autumn, place the planted container in a sheltered situation for a week before placing in its final position to acclimatise the plant. If the container is exposed and too heavy to move, keep the plants in their original pots for a few days in a sheltered place before planting up. However, we much prefer to buy a little later in the spring or earlier in the autumn in order to plant up immediately the plants are back home in the apartment.

5.5 Protection From the Hottest Suns, Coldest Winds and Driving Rain

Mediterranean weather is not always benign. By definition it means hot summers and cold winters. At times blistering hot and at times bitterly cold. So be prepared to protect your most tender plants when such weather arrives – normally with a warning. Even on a mild day the temperature variations can be amazing. On a typical mid-December day two blocks back from the beach the noon temperature surrounding plants in full sun in window boxes was 37 degrees C on the south side of a block of apartments and 21 degrees on the north side. At seven o'clock next morning it was 7 degrees in both places and plants were dripping with cold dew. In the summer they could have been 57 degrees and 33 degrees and 24 degrees in the morning.

THE HOTTEST SUNS

The most important things to do are as follows.

a. When you first plant up your plants ensure that you prepare a compost with a good water-holding capacity as described in Section 5.4.

b. Always pot up in impervious containers to prevent water evaporation through the sides.

c. Mulch the surface of the compost to reduce the speed of water evaporation from the surface. See page 120.

d. Install an awning or blind to shade plants not only from the high summer sun but also the low winter sun that comes into covered terraces affecting plants that have been in the shade all summer.

THE COLDEST WINDS

Many of the most populated areas of Spain lived in for the wonderful weather on most days of the year are down-wind from snowy mountains and ski resorts when cold winter gales blow from the north. Thermometers may not show temperatures below zero but the frost factor temperatures on the leaves of plants in exposed situations can be below zero as illustrated in the table.

Temperature on thermometer (ºC)	Wind speed around plants (km/hr)	Chill factor temp. on surface of leaves (ºC)
+2.5	0	+2.5
+2.5	8	0
+2.5	16	-5
+2.5	24	-7.5
0	0	0
0	8	-2.5
0	16	-7.5
0	24	-10
-2.5	0	-2.5
-2.5	8	-5
-2.5	16	-10
-2.5	24	-12.5
-10	0	-10
-10	8	-12.5
-10	16	-17.5
-10	24	-25

The damage that can be caused by wind chill factor temperatures is at three levels.

Level one: The burning browning and drying out of the tips of leaves and flowers. Typically at zero. Tropical/subtropical flowering plants die.

Level two: The burning browning and drying out of entire leaves. Typically at minus 2.5 degrees. Tropical fruit trees dying by now. Tender succulents severely burnt.

Level three: The freezing of the sap in leaves and branches. Typically at minus 5 degrees. Tropical fruit trees dead by this time. Many succulents die.

Level four: The freezing of fruit that turns black inside. Typically at minus 10 for citrus fruits, the trees themselves will die at minus 20 degrees..

Normally only exposed apartments are affected but in February 2005 freezing gales from the north and north-west created the lowest temperatures for 25 to 50 years, depending where you lived, and affected even the more benign corners of towns and cities from the Pyrenees to Gibraltar.

If you anticipate very cold conditions, the following precautions can be taken:

a. Avoid having plants affected by frosts in the first place. Plenty of alternatives are given in Section 4.2.

b. Move delicate plants inside, as is an annual event in places like Madrid.

c. Invest in a small vertical cold frame for smaller plants.

d. Wrap delicate plants in gardening fleece or bubble wrap, plant cosies and wraps.

e. Cut-off five and seven-litre empty water bottles that can be used as cloches with a cane through the top for stability.

f. Glaze part of your terrace and turn on a low-wattage, temperature-controlled, oil-filled heater.

g. Move succulents from outside exposed position to alongside windows and doors where there is always some heat loss.

h. Fit sliding glazed walls to the outside of the covered terrace for use when there are winter conditions.

DRIVING RAIN

The force of driving rain on apartment terraces and balconies can be greater than that in a garden enclosed by trees, high fences and hedges and the channelling of winds between apartment and nearby hotel and office blocks can result in plants being bashed by a wall of rain. So do take care what you plant on open terraces and the outer metre of covered terraces. Ensure that the weight of containers is sufficient to hold the plants in place and upright.

SALT SPRAY

Plants on front-line terraces and balconies can become coated with salt spray especially during storms. Many plants can be burnt and even killed by this, so ensure you plant the salt-resistant plants indicated in Section 4.2 and even then spray them with clean water after the storm.

5.6 Watering Your Plants

We would be millionaires if we had received a euro each time we answered the question "How much water should I give my plants?"

The theoretical answer is just sufficient to maintain the current size and rate of growth of each plant and replace the moisture lost by evaporation from the compost in which it is planted.

Unfortunately, as many plants suffer stress and even die due to over-watering as from under-watering.

Over-watering can be caused by:

a. Over-enthusiasm,

b. not turning off a drip irrigation system after rain,

c. co-planting thirsty and draught resistant plants in the same container and watering to keep the thirsty ones alive,

d. not cutting back watering in the autumn when the weather cools down,

e. watering rot-vulnerable plants such as cyclamens from the top rather than the bottom. The latter can be achieved by placing waterproof drip trays under pots and pouring water into the tray or placing the pot in a centimetre or two of water in a tray or bowl until it is soaked up.

f. not allowing the surface of the compost to dry out before watering again.

Under-watering can be caused by:

a. forgetfulness

b. poor compost with result that water runs straight through the container and insufficient water is retained

c. plants becoming root-bound so that water cannot get to the inner roots and the roots fill the entire container so little water enters

d. shallow watering not getting moisture down to the deeper nutrient and moisture-hunting roots. With taller roots the shallow roots can be the main guy ropes to keep the plant upright rather than being the main nutrient-gatherers,

e. not increasing watering in the spring as the weather warms up

f. being non-resident and not making provisions for the watering of permanently resident plants

In both cases not understanding whether each plant is by nature thirsty or not is a major problem. That is why we indicate this in the plant tables in Section 4.2.

In the cooler periods plant pots normally retain more moisture than you realise. Test this by lifting a few plants from their pots with the earth around their roots intact and then feel the compost and look at the state of a few roots. An inexpensive moisture metre is also useful in this respect.

In the hotter periods assume that moisture uptake and losses are high.
The more exposed to direct sunlight, the more mature the plant or tree and the greater natural thirstiness of a plant the more water that will be required. We have experienced 47 degrees C on both the Costa del Sol and Costa Blanca. Thirsty plants needed watering several times a day. Even when summer temperatures are more normal, around 35 degrees, annuals will need at least once and maybe twice — not only in sub-tropical areas of Andalusia but all over Spain.

If buying an apartment inland, recognise that the hottest places in Spain are not on the coast but around an hour or more inland. In Andalusia Seville is a record-breaking city and further north Xativa in the province of Valencia likewise.

Also summer temperatures in the north can be as hot as the south. When we walked for 50 days from the Bay of Biscay to the Med via the Pyrenees along the border between Spain and France we experienced temperatures over 35 degrees day after day in Navarra, Aragon and Cataluña as we progressed west to east from mid-June to early August. Amazingly, our last three days were the coolest with fresh snow on August 4 in the

Mediterranean foothills. But across the Pyrenees one sees almost only native plants, not imported sub and fully sub-tropical plants. When lush spring greenery on the mountainsides turns brown, native plants survive by putting down very deep roots. Something your plants cannot do in containers. So buy deeper containers for deeper-rooted plants such as bougainvillea, lantanas and trees next time you go out to buy some.

Having shared those experiences we recommend that in the summer months you need to add water to each container every other day in relation to the volume of the compost in the container. Trials we have carried out when the temperature was 35 degrees at midday and 25 during the night, with pots

Type of plant & weather	For thirsty plants				For drought-resistant plants			
	Hot summer***		Cool winter**		Hot summer**		Cool winter*	
Type of container	Full sun	Semi-shade	Full sun	Semi-shade	Full sun	Semi-shade	Full sun	Semi-shade
Pot – 20cm diameter	300ml	200ml	300ml	200ml	100ml	50ml	50ml	20ml
Pot – 40cm diameter	500ml	250ml	500ml	250ml	150ml	75ml	75ml	30ml
Window box – 10 litres	1000ml	700ml	1000ml	700ml	300ml	150ml	150ml	60ml
Tub – 40 litres	4 litres	3 litres	4 litres	3 litres	1.5 litres	750ml	750ml	300ml
Trough – 80 litres	8 litres	6 litres	8 litres	6 litres	3 litres	1.5 litres	1.5 litres	600ml
Volume of watering required: ***Every two days, ** Every week, * Every two weeks								

filled with a variety of purchased composts watered slowly with the same weight of moisture as compost, indicated that all the moisture had disappeared within 24 hours with no plants planted in the compost. The surface of the compost was not shaded by plants but equally no thirsty plant had drunk any of the water.

During the coming months try the watering guidelines of the table above and the ideas in the section that follows.

Note that it is preferable to water plants in the evening so that the water is soaked up by the compost with the minimum of evaporation loss and avoid wetting the leaves unless attempting to clean leaves after dirty rain. Many plants will grow healthier if watered with rain water rather than chlorinated tap water or water from a salt-based purifier.

If feasible, collect rainwater from a roof or using large funnels feeding into storage tanks. Very attractive tanks are now available as illustrated opposite. One on which plants could be stood to make it even more attractive.

5.7 Reducing Water Needs and Losses

A. QUALITY COMPOSTS
As discussed in Sections 5.3 and 5.4, always make sure you purchase or make up a compost that as well as being fertile retains water without becoming waterlogged.

B. MOISTURE-RETAINING GELS
As mentioned in Section 5.4, a soil-improving gel such as TerraCottem can be included in compost mixes or added to existing compost in pots by using a proprietary TerraCottem injection gun or sprinkling into deep holes made with a narrow trowel. Don't use more than the recommended dose of gel as otherwise the plants will rise out of the compost when watered.

C. IMPERVIOUS CONTAINERS

Buy containers manufactured with impervious materials or seal unsealed ones with a waterproofing paint before use.

D. MULCHING

Mulching involves covering the surface of the compost in containers with a material which will partially seal the surface so that less moisture will evaporate by surface evaporation and deeper capillary action. Also mulching will prevent the formation on the surface of composts in humid situations.

Suitable materials include:

• Half-centimetre layers of fine lava chippings

• A centimetre of larger crushed lava or reconstituted mini-lava balls

• River-worn stones – naturally or artificially coloured

• Hand-picked small rocks

• Black plastic sheeting covered with grit stones or compost

E. SLOW WATERING

Water slowly so that all the water is absorbed by the compost. Water in two or three stages if required.

F. DRIP TRAYS

Earthenware or plastic drip trays can be purchased to fit under pots, window boxes and

most other containers to catch excess water that runs out of the bottom of containers. This can be left to be sucked up as the container dries out or used to water an adjacent container.

G. LOOSENING SOIL SURFACE

Keep the top two centimetres of compost in un-mulched containers loose to prevent it baking hard and losing moisture by capillary evaporation.

H. VI-AQUA STIRRERS

The purchase of a small V-Aqua hand-held water-stirrer can help you improve the health of plants and at the same time reduce their watering needs. Full information about how this unit works and current prices are available from www.viaqua.ie. It has an official approval from Kew Gardens following its use in some of their greenhouses.

Use only the most drought resistant plants and mulch for minimum water losses.

5.8 Feeding Your Plants

Provided you planted your plants in a pre-fertilised compost you will not need to feed the plants for the first month for annuals and two or three months for perennials. This will encourage the root ball to grow searching for nutrients.

You then need to provide nutrients to top up what was in the original compost at the rate it is taken up and used up by the growing plant/s plus that flushed out of the compost by over-watering.

There are three ways of doing this.

▲ Adding a pearl to a pot

a. Placing a slow-release fertiliser pearl or stick into the soil as illustrated in the photograph. These normally provide six months nutrient supply for a small plant steadily growing plant. One plug would suffice for a year with a slow-growing plant. Two should therefore be used for medium-sized plants and three to five for large plants. Using such products means that you won't have to remember to make up a liquid feed or worry about getting the strength correct.

b. Placing granules of a slow-release fertiliser on the surface of the compost. This will be gradually dissolved when you water. Disadvantages are the need to get the dosage right and the coloured granules can look unsightly.

c. Adding a measure of a liquid fertiliser to the water when you water. Even if you make up the liquid accurately you won't use the same amount of water each time you water and you will loose some through the bottom of the container if it runs through.

This sort of feed is instantly available to the roots so they may be lazy and not spread searching through the compost. Over-feeding can result in fast, weak growth that is more susceptible to insect infestations and fungal attacks than healthier slower-growing plants.

d. Lookout for fertilisers high in potash for flowering plants and high in nitrogen for non-flowering evergreen plants.

5.9 Removing Dead Flowers to Stimulate New Flowers and Tidier Plants

The removal of dying and dead flowers from plants has several important benefits.

1. Flowering will be more continuous and longer for plants that normally flower over several or many months. The removal of dying flowers – called deadheading – stimulates the plant to quickly form new flower buds and then flowers in a second attempt to form seeds for natural reproduction that year. But be careful not to cut out the small forming buds. Your deadheading has cut short the natural sexual process of forming seeds. This is particularly important for plants such as cyclamen, geraniums and pelargoniums, petunias, margaritas etc.

2. For some plants that normally only flower once a year you might stimulate a second flowering and if plants normally only flower twice a year the gap between the first and second flowering will be shorter, as with plants such as roses.

3. Most bulbs such as irises, lilies and daffodils only flower once a year, but if you don't deadhead the plants and then leave the stalks and leaves to die back to strengthen the bulbs they may not flower the next year and indeed may wither and die after producing seeds. The bulbs will think that their lifetime mission of producing seeds is over.

4. Plants, especially those that only flower once or twice a year such as the herbs lavender, sage and rue, will look much tidier and neater if dead flowers and their stalks are cut off.

If you want to produce seeds for planting the next year, select a large strong flower and let it die and dry naturally. in the process creating a seed head enclosing many small seeds or one or two large ones. Harvest the dry seed pods, separate the seeds and give them a final drying in the sun, an oven or a proprietary tray dryer such as those manufactured by Stockli.

5.10 Removing Dead Leaves for Appearance and Health

Dead leaves appear on all plants from to time and on some more than others. Naturally deciduous plants will lose all their leaves every autumn/winter. These phenomena are part of the life cycle of a plant and dead leaves are best removed before they fall and, of course, remove any that fall and lie on the surface of the compost. If you leave them, they will start to rot down and could attract and harbour unwanted insects and slugs and snails in the restricted space. With more space in a garden and the countryside leaves will rot down and recycle nutrients to the soil but this process is restricted and takes a long time in the limited spaces of containers. Also container composts are likely to have less beneficial micro-organisms that help the recycling process than in a garden.

Naturally if the leaves of a plant start falling heavily before the autumn you have an unhealthy plant that needs urgent nursing or you will lose it. If this occurs, refer to Section 5.13.

5.11 Pruning to Keep Desired Size and Shape

As well as removing dead flower heads and leaves, trim dead stalks and untidy straggly growth. Also trim back plants that are starting to over-grow and starve less vigorous plants of light. If you are loath to trim certain foliage, move pots further from each other.

If you have plants in troughs, trim the sides to thicken them up and ensure they don't take up unnecessary terrace space. Trim them to a height related to your desire for privacy or maintaining views.

Pruning of fruit trees and plants is discussed in Section 8.8

5.12 Cleaning Your Plants

The leaves of plants, especially the shiny leaves of evergreen plants, can become dirty from three causes. Firstly, general dust that flies around when there is a breeze. Secondly, if exposed to dirty summer rains that carry a red dust from north Africa to the northerly Mediterranean shores. Thirdly, from the dust in the air from local construction or demolition sites. If the dirt film is allowed to build up, not only will the affected plants look unattractive but with the micro pores in the skin of the leaves blocked the vital process of photo synthesis will not be able to take place efficiently. The process of photosynthesis builds up the plants' nutrients and greening agents from carbon dioxide in the air.

You will find proprietary foliage cleaners for shiny-leafed plants in garden centres but we find it just as effective to first brush the leaves lightly with a soft paint brush and then wipe the leaves with a solution of milk and beer. These will remove any grime and give leaves a shine. If a plant was heavily affected and looks a little shaken after cleaning, spray the leaves with a proprietary foliar feed or a cooled nettle infusion. This is made by pouring one litre of boiling water on a dessertspoonful of dried nettle leaves. Cover and leave to cool. Then strain to use.

Dried nettle leaves can be purchased at a local health shop or herb stall in a weekly market.

We would normally avoid wetting the leaves of non-shiny plants when watering. But, if they become really grimy from dust rising from local construction work, they can be cleaned by putting under a shower or spraying with water.

5.13 Keeping Your Containers Clean

All pots, window boxes and other planted containers benefit from an twice-yearly external clean and also the insides when you empty them to change the compost before replanting. We suggest that you do this at the end of summer to remove summer dust and grime and at the end of winter to remove dirt grime and moss that can form, especially on the outside of terracotta pots.

Since there are delicate plant growth around avoid using chemical cleaners. Warm water with a few drops of ecological washing-up liquid should suffice for the end-of-summer clean. At the end of winter we suggest you clean pots, window boxes and containers with a solution of two tablespoons of vinegar in half a litre of water to clean off grime and algae.

5.14 Dealing with Pests and Diseases

In general, if you do not under or over-water and over-feed your plants — whether flowering plants, fruit trees or vegetables — you will minimise the occurrences of pest attacks and fungal diseases.

However, unfortunately, from time to time your plants can become affected by fungal spores, insects, snails and slugs and ants. Some may come in with the plants you buy and will appear fairly quickly while others may appear at any time. Even a plant 10 years of age may suddenly fail. The most common pests and diseases of the plants and trees — flowering fruit herbs and vegetables — you are likely to have on terrace, balcony or windowsill are grouped together for convenience in Part Ten. Here you are told what to look out for and how to deal with any problems.

5.15 Recuperating Unhealthy Plants

If plants look decidedly poorly with un-seasonal falling or drooping of leaves and the drying up of flower buds, you obviously have an unhealthy plant.

You have two options: remove and replace the plant or, if it is the only plant in a container, move the problem pot or container to a nursery area out of the sun.

There will be six main reasons for the ill health of the plant.

a. You have over-watered the plant causing the roots and bottom of stems to become waterlogged and rot. In this case you can let the plant almost dry out and then water very lightly with water to which a fungicide such as propolis has been added to keep the soil just damp and see if the plant recovers, but this has a low probability.

b. You have watered erratically or under-watered the plant, forgotten all together for a few days due to work visitors or a hectic social calendar. A gentle watering increasing over a couple of days may enable the plant to recover. But don't forget next time the plant is unlikely to be as forgiving. If this becomes a regular occurrence, revisit Part Four and plant drought-resistant plants such as succulents many of which have delightful although not long-lasting flowers. The falling off of lower leaves is often a sign of under-watering.

c. You have over-watered and over-fed or just over-fed the plant, causing fast but weak growth that can be vulnerable to fungal and insect attacks. If you think that this is what you have done, stop the feeding, cut back the watering by a half and add a fungicide to the water and if you see signs of insect attacks treat as advised in Section 5.12. You will find photographs of typical fungal and insect attacks to help you identify and treat problems in this section.

d. If variegated-leaved plants are in darkish places for too long they can revert to green. This can be reverted by placing them in a better light.

e. Brown patches can be caused on green-leaved plants by being in too much sunlight and drying winds. Mist-spraying can help plants recover.

5.16 A Terrace Tool Kit

Naturally you will need a few tools to look after even a few pots and a window box and a few more if you have extensive plantings. But — even for the most active apartment gardener — the essential tool kit is not extensive or expensive. We indicate below what we regard as the minimum and maximum needs.

A BASIC TOOL KIT

All the beginner and experienced gardener with just a few pots and containers needs whatever they are growing are the following:

1. An old kitchen fork or a hand fork

2. An old table spoon or a trowel

3. An old knife or a forked dibber.

4. A pair of kitchen scissors or a light pruning tool or secateurs.

5. A kitchen jug or a long-spouted watering can for watering.

6. A kitchen broom and dustpan for sweeping the terrace which you do anyway.

7. A pair of gardening or plastic gloves for use when mixing composts and filling containers.

A FULL SET OF TOOLS

If you intend to lay out, or already have, a full-scale terrace garden all you really need in addition are the following:

8. If plant pots have been hung on walls or placed on the top of walls above two metres, a 250cc tilting can on the end of a pole will make watering easier than balancing on a ladder. You may well have seen these on poles extendable up to four metres in some of the geranium-filled patio gardens open to the public during Spain's annual May Patio Festival in Córdoba.

9. A bucket for standing pots in for bottom watering. See Section 5.6

10. A small soft paintbrush for loosening and removing dust from plant leaves especially shiny, smooth evergreen leaves.

11. Four separate hand-sprayers dedicated to an insecticide, a fungicide, a foliar feed and water for a final wash of foliage covered in dust.

12. A large builders/gardeners black plastic basket/bucket for mixing composts in.

13. An old sock or stocking for shaking yellow sulphur powder over summer fruit vegetables such as tomatoes and peppers and a grape vine if planted.

14. The Vi-Aqua water stirrer improver mentioned in Section 5.7.

15. For the scientist in the family a hand-held moisture and Ph metre may be interesting. It is fascinating to realise that soil only just damp to the touch actually holds a substantial amount of water. If you suspect that the death of most of the plants on your terraces is due to over or under-watering, a moisture metre would be a timely birthday or Christmas present.

16. If you are building up a collection, a packet of plastic name labels and a water-resistant marker for writing the names. It is so easy to forget names just as you are explaining what you have to a friend.

Types of containers for terraces, balconies and windowsills

Pleasurable plant displays require a three-way match between plants, pots and position in your apartment. Each need to be right for each other and in harmony with your overall vision and plan for terraces, balconies and windowsills. As was explored in Part Four, there is a wide choice of plants to choose from and equally a wide range of containers. To help you make informed choices, we describe the containers available and their main uses and shortcomings.

6.1 Introduction

The photographs and plans presented in Parts Two and Three highlighted the many types of plants and containers available and the importance of getting the combinations right and also appropriate to the overall design and location of your apartment. Indeed the pleasure you will get from your terraces, balconies and windowsills will be related to the interrelationships between plants, pots and the positions in which they are placed.

The choice of suitable containers is amazing and expands each year. They are available in a wide range of shapes, sizes, materials, textures and colours. Shapes vary from the original round pot to square tubs, oblong window boxes and troughs, trays to growing tables and from stylish urns to amphoras.

Materials used to make containers have expanded from the terracotta and ceramic pots turned on a potter's wheel or pressed on volume production lines to moulded and pressed plastics and concrete, fibre glass, wood, tin, copper, galvanised steel, aluminium, stone and even a rice husk resin mix. Very importantly, modern technology enables a plastic container to have an external finish indistinguishable from genuine terracotta and it will be considerable less weighty. Also many containers now have inbuilt water reservoirs which makes it easier to maintain compost at a constant moisture level.

The influence of interior designers is evident in the wide range of subtle and garish colours, tints and hues and the variety of moulded and printed designs. There are now even double-skinned transparent tubs of various colours that light up giving a special effect to plants in the tub and the surrounding area.

Regarding the colour to use for containers there are three choices.

1. Keep things simple and use one colour.

2. Be bold and go for something bright like a row or group of red or orange ones. If living in a studio apartment, you could go way out for a kaleidoscope effect with pots of all colours in sequence with matching flower colours to reinforce the effect.

3. Use ceramic containers with brightly coloured designs. Mediterranean flower motifs can be attractive especially in coastal areas. But don't end up with pots and tubs that become the focal point rather than the plants with in them. However, if this is what you want consider instead using empty decorated pots to brighten up the terrace. But don't end up with a mishmash of designs unless you plan to collect pots.

We discuss the colour mixing of plants in Section 4.5 (Having fun with colour mixing). The same concepts apply to pots and in practice the two things are intertwined.

With many mature plants their containers will be partially or fully covered by foliage so save money and buy plain containers for most plants.

Look around to see what is available locally and buy according to how subdued or lively you wish your displays of planted and empty containers to be. Displays in garden centres and ceramic shops are like an Aladdin's cave, with new treasures on every square metre of shelf and floor space. You can just add a few potted plants or turn your terrace into a luxurious outdoor living space that might become the most used room of the apartment.

We give a brief description of a wide range of useful containers and their various potential uses in Section 6.2. Section 6.3 indicates how mass-produced commercial products can be modified by apartment owners without a major investment in materials or time. If you are a professional potter or attending a pottery course, you could make your own.

When choosing containers take into account and achieve a balance between the following factors.

a. Size – Is it large enough not to have to re-pot the plant you intend to buy within a couple of years?

b. Shape – Do you want to keep to one general shape in various sizes or mix compatible shapes?

c. Surface design – You will see it with upright growing plants or if you intend to keep it empty but in many cases cascading greenery will hide the design.

d. Colour – Bright or subdued? Single or mixed colours?

e. Self-watering – Very useful but sometimes expensive.

f. Materials – Will the materials last? Thin terracotta can break if knocked. Terracotta/glass fibre mesh containers look very stylish and are light but fall apart after a couple of years. Wood looks great new but soon weathers due to moisture seepage.

g. Weight – Will you be able to move them and will they be heavy enough not to fall over on a windy terrace?

h. Wheels – If a container is heavy, are wheels built-in or can a support with castors be fitted underneath?

An expanding range of materials and finishes are available from Mediterranean and other countries, but we believe that for most positions there is still nothing to beat traditional terracotta containers if first sealed or today's terracotta plastic imitations. And for most balconies and apartment terraces the latter win from the point of view of weight.

But choices are personal preferences so read on and reflect on your own.

6.2 An A to Z of the Types of Useful Containers

A SMALL PLANT POTS AND TUBS

What is round we refer to as a pot and what is square we refer to as a tub. We consider pots and tubs up to 20cm wide and 20cm high as being small. This is the width of an A4 sheet of paper.

The type of container one would use for:

• a single small/medium sized plant, or

• two or three smaller plants for placing on a windowsill, sideboard, table, pot support column or stepped display stand/plant theatre or placed as a line at the front or back of a balcony or terrace.

• producing new plants from cuttings or potting on seedlings from germinating trays. In a greenhouse one would often use smaller pots for this purpose but apartment terraces can be windy and like an oven at times and compost dries out quickly.

When choosing pots or tubs, recognise that the prime disadvantages of the plain terracotta and plastic varieties. The former are heavy and won't blow around in the wind, but they soon lose moisture by evaporation especially in the hotter months. The latter, while waterproof, can bounce around in the wind if the compost is allowed to dry out.

But there some simple solutions. Paint the inside of terracotta pots with a waterproofing paint and place the plastic ones inside a heavier and better looking terracotta or ceramic pot or tub. In practice we suggest you do not use pots and tubs less than 15cm wide or deep, otherwise you will be continually watering the plants as the small amount of compost they contain can only retain small volumes of water that will be inadequate in hot weather.

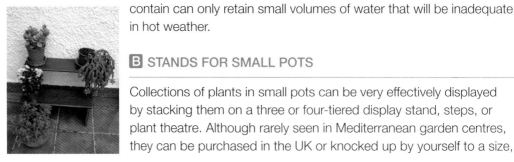

B STANDS FOR SMALL POTS

Collections of plants in small pots can be very effectively displayed by stacking them on a three or four-tiered display stand, steps, or plant theatre. Although rarely seen in Mediterranean garden centres, they can be purchased in the UK or knocked up by yourself to a size, design and colour that looks best in your situation. Units can be made or purchased to place against walls or in corners.

C WALL POTS

Attractive terracotta and ceramic wall pots are available. Since they hold little composts and drip when watered, they are best used for drought-resistant succulents, especially on open terraces. Recently a multi-plastic wall pot has been launched in the UK that consists of three tiers of three plastic pots joined together to a plastic backing sheet. A great idea for a small herb bed by the door to the terrace. Until they become available in your area it's easy to make one by using a thick sheet of plastic, nine 10cm-wide plastic tubs and instant glue.

D RECYCLED PLASTIC WATER BOTTLES

Bottles of 500ml and 1.5 litre size, with their tops cut off, are very useful for growing new plants from cuttings and in blocks of six for growing deep-rooted vegetables such as leeks. Bottles of five and seven litres are useful for raising plants from seeds. As illustrated, don't cut the top totally off but leave a hinge. It can then be pulled down to act as a cloche until plants are hardened off. If you cut off the bottom of these larger bottles you can use them as cloches on raised beds and growing tables when growing vegetables.

E MEDIUM-SIZED POTS AND TUBS

Pots and tubs from 25cm to 45cm height and width we regard as medium. They include plain round and square and also small-sized traditional urns and amphoras. Sometimes they are partially glazed with a brown or green which can be an attractive touch. The main uses will be to plant:

a. Individual flowering and evergreen perennial plants.

b. Small groups of annuals and bulbs.

c. Small collections of succulents and cacti.

d. Flowering and fruiting trees.

e. Flowering and fruiting vines.

f. Individual tomato pepper and aubergine plants.

g. Small sowings or plantings of vegetables.

Medium-sized pots can also be placed on top of plinths for decorative purposes.

F WHEELS FOR HEAVY POTS AND TUBS

Even medium-sized pots and tubs filled with damp compost and plants can be heavy to move around. Even impossible if one lacks physical strength. Fortunately some are now supplied with built-in wheels or separate supports with castors. The latter are placed underneath before filling the containers. If you cannot trace either or they are too expensive for your budget, the wheels sold to place under gas bottles are an inexpensive solution. DIY pot/tub supports are easy to make.

G VERY LARGE POTS AND TUBS

There are plastic, glass fibre, terracotta and concrete pots and tubs up to 1.5 metres in height and width. Rather impractical for anything other than a large, open terrace — especially penthouse terraces.
Used for planting large trees such as palms and olive, preparing mini-gardens with a mix of drought-resistant plants with the sides draped in trailing plants, a water feature and as a raised bed for growing vegetables.

H WINDOW BOXES

Ceramic, terracotta and plastic window boxes are available. The most practical for placing on windowsills, balconies and hanging on the front balustrade or railings of a terrace are plastic ones with a built-in water reservoir.
This reduces the weight of compost filled window boxes when you want to lift them into place or move when re-potting and considerably reduces the frequency and time required for watering them. Without a built-in reservoir you could be watering once or twice a day in mid-summer and every few days or week in the winter depending on what you are planting.
They come in lengths from 30 to 90cm and with depths and widths of 15 to 20cm.
If you plan to plant small squat or taller growing plants, ceramic window boxes with interesting designs may be of interest. However, if you plan to plant trailing plants that will

soon cover the sides of the window boxes plain coloured boxes are less fussy and often less expensive.

Often you have will have brown, terracotta, green, white and, increasingly, a wider range of colours to choose from. Test several possible colours with plants before investing in your boxes. Terracotta, black and green often blend in well with black railings and green with many colours of balustrade wall and each better than the brown colour of many window boxes. But the chose of colours is according to personal taste.

■ LARGE TROUGHS OR PLANTERS

Fifty centimetre to one-and-a-half-metre long troughs or planters are available in various depths and widths from 25 to 40 centimetres. Can be made in plastic, wood, metal, glass fibre and ceramics. They can be considered to be large or even giant window boxes but too heavy to hang on railings. Unless you use plastic versions they may be too heavy for many balconies and the sheer effort required to transport a lead or concrete one in a lift or worse up several flights of stairs makes them impractical. Can be used to plant a long display of annuals or perennial plants and can also be used for a strawberry or vegetable bed like a long and narrow raised bed. You could also plant a hedge to screen you from neighbouring apartments or a facing apartment block or local eyesore. Cypresses, canes, trimmed bottle brush, mandarin and lavender plantings come to mind.

Best purchased or made with castor wheels for moving around. For instance you might want to park a hedge across a terrace during the day as a divider between the sitting/eating and clothes drying areas and place alongside railings in front of the eating area at night for privacy.

Trellis can also be added to planters for supporting perfumed flowering climbers and climbing beans if growing vegetables. The unit shown can be easily knocked up by a handy person especially if a local carpenter pre-cuts the wood.

■ BUILT-IN PLANTERS

Some apartments and penthouses will have planters built-into the fabric of the building by the builder. The advantages of these is that they are often deep enough for the root balls of large plants, even trees. The walls can be pleasingly covered by trailing plants.

The major disadvantage is that they sometimes leak and cause problems for the surrounding tiles or even a lower apartment. We suggest that you therefore paint them inside with a water sealant membrane to seal the base and side walls before filling with composts and planting up.

K BONSAI TRAYS

If you intend to develop a collection of bonsai plants you will need to buy the specially produced shallow ceramic trays and every few years replant your developing bonsais into larger trays to house the wider spreading roots required to support to growth of a bonsai until it reaches it's optimum size.

The larger sizes of bonsai trays can also be planted attractively with a collection of small cacti or used to construct a micro garden. Apparently these used to be popular in some Mediterranean countries before the advent of relatively inexpensive cut flowers and house plants.

L BLACK PLASTIC TRAYS

The 8cm-deep, 55cm-long, 40cm-wide black plastic trays sold in horticultural supply shops and agricultural cooperatives have several uses including the following.

a. To stand potted plants in two centimetres of water for beneficial bottom watering.

b. As the container for a miniature garden or Nativity scene which are popular in Spain. Decades ago miniature gardens were taken to cemeteries instead of expensive cut flowers on All Soul Day.

c. To hold a collection of small plants.

d. To keep pots with seedlings or cuttings tidy and to make it easy to water them by placing a piece of horticultural blanket on base of the tray and keeping it always damp.

e. As a seed tray if you decide to grow flowering plants and vegetable plantlets from seeds for transplanting when sizeable or micro vegetables such as mustard and cress and perilla (shiso) leaves. The latter are cut when harvested rather than eating the whole seedling as with sprouting seeds.

Empty fish boxes are roughly the same size and can be used for the same purposes.

M HERB, STRAWBERRY AND POTATO BARRELS

1. Herb and strawberry barrels

Various sizes of plastic, terracotta and wood barrels with numerous holes for planting strawberry or herb plants are available. The plastic ones often look just like terracotta these days and have the advantage of not loosing moisture by evaporation through the walls which is a potential problem with terracotta barrels unless painted internally with a paint

water proofing paint. Also moss builds up less on the plastic surface than on terracotta.

This type of barrel tends to come in two shapes with bowed sides and straight sides. They take up little space on a sunny or semi-shaded balcony or terrace and can be stood on the ground, a wide wall, a pedestal or a table or side board. A row on a balcony would produce greater crops than a single or pair of barrels one for strawberries and one for herbs.

Wooden barrels can look authentic and stylish on a larger terrace but suffer from looking damp after a while and eventually rotting. As with terracotta it is best to seal the inside with a water proofing paint before filling with a suitable compost.

2. Potato Barrels

We used to grow new potatoes in a medium-sized plastic barrel, but now specially designed barrels are available. Two versions are illustrated. The first is a wicker barrel into which a heavy-duty plastic sack, available from www.harrodhorticulture.com, is inserted. The second is a double plastic tube, the outer one sliding up to enable the first potatoes to be harvested from the bottom and then progressively upwards as they form by sliding the tube higher. This is available from www.organiccatalog.com. Both can be stood on a black plastic tray for cleanliness.

N WOODEN BARRELS FOR PLANTS AND TREES

Complete quarter, half or full-size barrels can be obtained from some wine bodegas and garden centres. The quarter size are useful for planting trees and shrubs on open medium-sized terraces. The half and full-sized barrels are only for large terraces. Grape vines look authentic growing in a wine barrel. Also useful for major displays of flowering plants.

O GROW BAGS

Although popular for decades in northern Europe, they have only recently reached Spain. Typically 80cm long by 30cm wide and containing 25 litres of compost with marked planting holes ready to cut out, they are a convenient size for a few tomato pepper and aubergine plants or a bed of lettuces or Swiss chard. Indeed, Floragard are now marketing red grow bags for fruit vegetables and green bags for leaf vegetables each with ecological natural

fertilisers appropriate to each family of vegetables mixed into the composts.

Grow bags can be grown on the ground or on the top of a table or sideboard covered with a plastic sheet or tablecloth. They could also be used for courgettes and even a squash plant plus a wide range of shallow-rooted flowering plants in a penthouse terrace landscape. If you can't trace grow bags, a 25, 50 or 80-litre bag of good fertilized compost with holes cut in the top can be used in the same way. See page 215 for a supplier.

P GROWING TABLES

Growing tables are becoming popular for the growing of vegetables on covered terraces. In Spain they are being referred as *huertos urbanos* (urban allotments). They can also be used on open terraces but one needs to construct a mini plastic tunnel over the table or provide for drainage to prevent the compost becoming waterlogged and the plants suffering. The advantage of growing tables is that they provide a sizeable growing area and the legs can be anything from 30cm to a metre high depending on whether you prefer to sit on a low or high chair, or stand to work the micro vegetable plot. The growing table illustrated was made by our local carpenter in marine quality plywood and is 20cm deep and 70cm by 100cm in growing area. It has castors on the legs so that it can be wheeled around. If we had not been writing this book, we would have made it ourselves. It could easily be knocked up by a handy person on an apartment terrace getting the wood pre-cut by a wood supply shop. Naturally you can make to a size that best suits the space you have. An optimum width for working from one side is 80cm and from two sides 150cm. A number of companies now supply growing tables manufactured in wood, aluminium and galvanised steel (see the Useful Addresses page for a supplier).

Growing tables are convenient for the following without backache as you can sit on a stool to work or stand without bending far.

- Growing vegetables.
- Housing collections of cacti succulents and other plants.
- As a potting table.
- Enthusiasts could construct a mini garden even with a small-scale train running through it.
- Propagating new plants from cutting or seeds for own use swapping or sale

All your tools and fertilisers etc could be stored in a plastic box below.

6

Q RAISED BEDS

If you take the legs off a growing table, one immediately has a raised bed 20cm-deep, which is sufficient for growing most vegetables. Plastic and woven plastic fabric ones are also available.

This concept of an oblong or square box can obviously be expanded to any length and a width of 1.5 metres if your terrace space allows for working from both sides. You could also increase the depth to 30cm for growing deeper-rooted plants. Constructing a raised bed with a frame and a black plastic liner covering the sides and base is easy and less expensive than purchasing one with a solid base.

Although we talk of growing vegetables a raised bed can also be used to:

- Grow a mass display of flowering plants.
- Establish a strawberry bed – preferably wild strawberries for taste.
- Build up collections of plants such as herbs, cacti and bonsais. There is more information regarding plant collections in Section 4.8.

A number of Europe-wide mail order distributors of gardening products offer both wooden and plastic raised beds with mini plastic tunnels. The most widely known are probably www.harrodhorticulture.com and www.organiccatalog.com.

The disadvantage of raised beds compared to growing tables is that you will need to kneel or bend down to work on it while with a growing table you can stand or sit on a stool seat or wheel chair. This problem can be reduced to an extent by adding legs.

R PLASTIC STORAGE BOXES

Inexpensive plastic storage boxes are available in many stores including the Chinese stores that have taken over most of the traditional Spanish "100 peseta" shops.

The ones in the photograph are 25cm high by 30cm. They are very convenient for growing a wide assortment of vegetables. Twelve boxes side by side are equivalent to a one square metre raised bed.

S BUILDERS/GARDENERS PLASTIC BUCKETS

The photograph shows two typical sizes of plastic basket. Both are excellent for growing all types of vegetables especially those with deep roots such as globe artichokes, horseradish, parsnips and sweet potatoes. Can also be used for fruit trees and bushes and flowering shrubs. Good for making up compost mixes.

T HANGING BASKETS AND POTS

Hanging baskets and pots are not as popular in a Mediterranean climate as in temperate zone situations due to the speed at which they dry out when the sun is hot — which is most of the year. If you are prepared to water twice a day or install a timer-controlled irrigation system by all means have a go, but we prefer to restrict the use of hanging baskets to semi-shaded open areas as they drip when watered which one would not want in a dry, covered terrace. We would rather use waterproof hanging pots if there is room on the terrace without knocking ones head.

Also rather than plant trailing petunias or portulacas consider trailing succulents that need infrequent watering. You will find hanging pots for fixing to ceilings and walls in the garden centres, gardening sections of do-it-your-self stores and ceramic shops.

A recent development is specially designed hanging planters for growing tomato plants upside down. They are very space-saving. See section 3.7.

U LIVING WALL POUCHES

In recent years living wall pouches have become popular in the UK and other northern European countries but are rarely seen in the Mediterranean countries. They are hung on a wall and small plants are grown in a rich compost placed in each pouch. Typical plantings include a collection of small herb plants, annuals such as petunias and nasturtiums and small vegetables such as red lettuces. Best hung in the semi-shade they can be an alternative wall hanging to painting, ceramic plates or glazed murals.

V ROCKERY TRAYS

Large plastic trays can be commissioned as the base for a rockery on a large terrace especially on a penthouse terrace. Planted with succulents or cacti they will not require much watering or maintenance.

W FLOWER BED TRAYS AND FRAMES

Flower and herb beds can be created on similar trays or on a plastic sheet raised up and fixed to a wooden or plastic surround as illustrated. Useful on medium and large terraces.

X PREFORMED PONDS

Preformed plastic or glass fibre ponds in various sizes and with surrounding hollows for planting plants are available in many garden centres and DIY stores. Can be accommodated on medium and large terraces.

Y PLASTIC BOWLS

Basic plastic washing up or plastic or ceramic mixing bowls can be used to create mini ponds surrounded by a few rocks hiding potted plants. They can also be planted an interesting selection of small plants perhaps with flowers matching the colour of the bowl. Bowls are also very useful for planting groups of spring summer winter or autumn bulbs.

Z PREFORMED LANDSCAPES

Some garden centres now stock glass fibre and plastic preformed rocks and landscapes to go round ponds. These can be used on large terraces especially roof tops as they are light to create a range of tidy landscapes. Most towns will have a glass fibre-forming company which could produce your own landscape design. Plants can be planted in pots fixed into the formed landscape and trailing plants and stone and lava chippings can soon soften the harshness of the raw landscape. Alternatively you could obtain a preformed landscape in a sandy colour and rough gritty finish and plant up with cacti to create a desert landscape or in a green colour and plant up with ground cover plants which would eventually cover most of the green glass fibre surface.

6.3 Modifying Basic Products to Better Meet Your Needs

As now illustrated there are an amazing number of container products and designs available for you to purchase to enhance terraces, balconies and windowsills. But in most cases their production has moved from hand-made to mass production over the past 30 years.

Designs have been become more and more driven by production constraints and designers' ideas of what the average garden centre wishes to stock rather than the preferences of end-user customers who will look at the containers day after day, perhaps for the rest of their lives.

If one hunts around there are some brilliant container products available, but there are also some that make one wonder who would ever buy them. If you are determined that those on your terraces, balconies and windowsills are unique it is relatively easy to modify commercial containers of all sizes and designs.

The following are some easy transformations.

a. Paint the containers in a bright or subdued colour that exactly matches your vision of what is right for your windowsill, balcony and terrace.

b. Changing/softening the texture of harsh-looking containers by coating/painting them with a course sand cement mix or a peat cement or water proof glue mix and then painting.

c. Sticking clay or plastic motifs on containers and then painting them.

d. Adhering sea shells to the outside of containers.

e. Highlighting added or the original raised motifs on commercial containers with a different colour paint.

6.4 Conclusion

As you can see you are spoilt for choice. There is something for every situation, type size and colour of plant, colour scheme, shape of terrace balcony and windowsill. Beyond the above list we have seen interesting displays of plants in things like an old dentist chairs, wheel barrows, large watering cans, the cover for an inflatable life boat etc. Combine this choice of containers with the information about plants in Part Four and your terraces, balconies and windowsills will look great.

Growing culinary and medicinal herbs

Herbs make good plants for containers as they are attractive, often relatively drought and frost-resistant, improve the taste of food, have beneficial health properties and are perfumed. Thus they create natural aroma-therapeutic effects throughout the year.

7.1 Why Grow Herbs?

THE HERITAGE OF HERBS

The Mediterranean region is the natural home of many herbs. Some have always been here and others came with traders from the Middle East, and from the Moors when they moved into the Iberian peninsula. Others arrived from South America and, more recently, additional varieties and types have been added by seed collectors and by imports from international seed catalogues.

From the Middle Ages onwards collections were built up in royal, monastery and medicinal gardens and then, as the art of cooking and preparing healthy beverages developed, culinary gardens grew up to the stage where few gardens around villas did not include herbs.

Today they are also becoming popular for flower pot and window box collections on apartment window ledges, balconies and terraces.

REASONS FOR POPULARITY OF HERBS

There are many reasons for this increasing interest in growing herbs in apartment containers.

1. Many have attractive foliage and flowers.

2. Many are perennials and are not particularly thirsty plants.

3. Many are annuals that are relatively easy to care for and grow from seed. See Section 4.10.

4. Many are noticeably aromatic so their oils add a pleasant smell to a terraceenvironment. Because of this they tend not to be invaded by insects as their perfumes act as an insect repellent.

5. Many can be harvested from a terrace for use in recipes of all kinds.

6. Many infusions using fresh herbs are relaxing, invigorating and help one prevent or overcome basic ailments. See Section 7.7.

7. They can be grown in all the types of containers considered in Part Six.

8. They offer one of the easiest possibilities for building up an interesting and useful plant collection focussed not only on types of herbs but also varieties of a given type. Mints, basil and sages are among those that could lend themselves to building up a family collection as discussed in Section 4.8.

9. It's a way of preserving native plants in the urban environment.

10. They are interesting plants for those with impaired sight, who can pick, smell, feel and taste the leaves and flowers.

7.2 Where and in What Can They Be Grown?

Herbs can be grown almost anywhere provided you differentiate in selecting and locating them between the perennial herbs that are fairly drought-resistant and the thirsty annual herbs that are best not exposed to the hot summer suns, and you don't buy non frost-resistant herbs if you have winter frosts.

Typical locations and types of containers are as follows.

- Anywhere in Spain and other Mediterranean climate locations.
- Low-growing herbs can look good on windowsills if not too frequently harvested.
- On balconies a collection can be built up in ceramic or plastic herb pots as illustrated and also in troughs, window boxes (see section 4.5), a row of pots along the front or back of the balcony or in a tiered pot stand to minimise the floor space required and produce an interesting feature.

- Small and medium-sized plants for culinary and medicinal harvesting can be grown on walls in ceramic wall pots, a block of plastic pots, a tier of short window boxes and wall pouches.
- Herbs look good grown in groups on terraces. Either in groups of pots on the floor or on a table conveniently by the door into the apartment or as individual specimens in medium-sized pots among flowering plants.
- On larger terraces a collection could be grown in a raised bed, growing table, large trough or rockery.
- Containers of herbs around tubs of vegetables or a growing table can give that area an enhanced appearance (see Section 9.1 B) and herbs for the kitchen can be harvested at the same time as vegetables.

If grown in pots and window boxes, they are easy to move around to the most suitable summer and winter microclimates.

7.3 What Are the Best Herbs for Beginners?

The list presented below is chosen on the basis of the following criteria.

- A good selection of plants can be easily obtained from garden centres.
- Seeds can be obtained easily from garden centres and international mail order catalogues (see Section 9.1 B). See Useful Addresses at the end of the book)
- Readers are likely to harvest them for culinary and health uses.

- If a perennial, they are reasonably easy to grow from cuttings.
- If an annual, they are relatively easy to grow from seed.
- They are relatively easy to care for throughout the year.
- Grown in containers, they do not become too large for small terraces.
- The plants are in the main noticeably aromatic.

We would advise you to start by buying small plants and later move on to growing from seed, especially to build up a collection of different varieties. For instance we grow six varieties of basil and two types of coriander – one best for leaves and the other for seeds.

A BAKER'S DOZEN OF BEGINNERS' HERBS FOR APARTMENT GROWING.

1. Parsley/*perijil*. Annual. Best to buy a plant for a couple of years and then try seeds. Spanish plants tend to be coarser than the several fine-leafed varieties one can grow from seed but tend to be slow to germinate. Moderately easy. Best in semi-shade.

2. Sage/*salvia*. Perennial. Best to buy a plant. Buy the basic, grey-leaved common variety, *salvia officinalis*. Later you can experiment with other varieties from seed, especially if you have a large terrace. There are more than 800 varieties world-wide but many are not frost-resistant. Easy. Sun or semishade.

3. Thyme/*tomillo*. Perennial. You will probably come across green and green and yellow variegated varieties. Best to buy plants. Can rot off if waterlogged. Moderately easy. Likes sun.

4. Mint/*menta*. Perennial. A number of varieties with different leaves and flavours normally available. A mixed mint collection can be pleasing. Try a leaf before buying a plant. Can die back in the winter. Moderately easy. Sun or semi-shade.

5. Chives/*cebollinos*. Perennial. Buy a plant if you can find one. If not grow from seed. Will probably die back for two or three months in the winter. Easy. Sun or semi-shade.

6. Basil/*albahaca*. Annual. Wide range of varieties. Common plant buy, grow others from seed. Moderately easy. Sun or semi-shade.

7. Bay/*laurel*. Perennial. Buy plant. Can trim to keep small or grow as a metre high trimmed bush either side of the window on a balcony. Easy. Sun, semi-shade or shade.

8. Lemon verbena/*hierba Luisa*. Small perennial shrub. Keep trimmed to size you want. A pleasant summer infusion hot or cold. Buy plant. Very scented foliage and flowers. Easy. Sun and semi-shade.

9. Garlic/*ajo*. Annual. Grow for the young stalks. Plant a 30 or 40cm pot with cloves 2cm apart in the autumn. Good for you and tastes good in salads and omelettes. Moderately easy. Sun and semi-shade.

10. Marjoram/*orégano*. Perennial. Suggest you buy a plant of the bushy green-leaved variety but have a go at growing from seed the low-growing gold (oro) variety that is rarely

found in garden centres. Easy. Sun or semi-shade.

11. Rue/*ruda.* Perennial. Interesting yellow flowers as well as grey-green foliage. Trim to shape to stop it going leggy. Some persons are allergic to it. Easy. Sun or semi-shade.

12. Rosemary/*romero.* Trailing variety. Perennial. Keep trimmed to shape. Moderately easy. Sun and semi-shade.

13. Lemon balm/*Melisa.* Perennial. Easy. Perfumed leaves. Cut back to new growth when it starts to get straggly. Buy a plant or grow from seed. Semi-shade.

7.4 What Other Herbs can be Added on Large Terraces?

If you have a large terrace or rooftop, we suggest adding the following larger growing herb plants to your plant collection. They will individually and jointly add some spectacular plants and foliage. Some flowers and leaves are tasty in salads and others have culinary and wellness benefits.

1. Rosemary. Perennial. Bush varieties can be added to the trailing variety. Buy small plants as it will be easier to get a good root ball established. Keep well trimmed to stop growing leggy. Moderately easy. Sun and semi-shade.

2. Pineapple sage/*elegana rutilans.* Perennial. The small plant you will buy can grow into a clump filling a medium and even large pot in a few years. It will become a very attractive — indeed impressive — plant. Would look great on a large terrace or balcony alongside the following plant. Flowers and young leaves edible in salads. Sun.

3. Velvet sage/*Salvia leucantha.* Perennial. As plant above. See the photograph of both together. Not edible. Easy. Sun.

4. Lavander/*lavanda* or *lavandula.* Perennial. A number of varieties with different forms of leaves and flowers will be found in good garden centres. Give a good perfume to balconies and terraces – might even attract passing butterflies. Easy. Sun or semi-shade.

5. Coriander /*cilantro.* Annual. Grow from seed for both the leaves and seeds which are used in many recipes. Can go to seed quickly so if you especially want the leaves look out for a variety of seeds that is slow to bolt. Not the easiest but try. Semi-shade.

6. Garlic bulbs/*ajo.* Perennial or annual. With more space young garlic can be allowed to mature to produce garlic bulbs for the kitchen. Can be planted in pots of flowering plants or alongside other vegetables grown on the terrace. If allowed to go to seed – especially the giant varieties found in France – the flowers are interesting and the smell keeps insects away from surrounding plants. Easy. Sun.

7. Rocket/*oruga*. Annual. Grow from seed in an individual container or as a block on a growing table. Gives a special taste to salads. Easy. Trim off top growth when starts to form flower buds. Semi-shade or sun.

9. Tarragon/*estragón*. Perennial. Buy plant and pot up in medium-sized pot or a larger container as part of a collection. Easy. Semi-shade or sun.

10.Dill/*eneldo*. Annual. Buy a plant but you will have more to use if you grow from seed in a medium-sized container or on a growing table. Moderately easy. Semi-shade.

11. Purslane/*verdelaga*. Annual. Green and golden-leaved varieties available. Healthy addition to salads as reported to have a useful level of Omega 3. Easy. Sun and semi-shade.

12.Stevia/*stevia rebaudiana*. Perennial. Will over-winter if you keep container just damp in an inner corner of the terrace and move part of the day to a semi-shaded/sun-only position as quite thirsty once it sprouts in the spring. Be careful not to over-water as roots can rot. Best propagated from cuttings every two years. A natural sweetener discovered in Paraguay by Spanish conquerors but never became popular as Spain was experiencing a mini ice age that continued to the first half of the 19th century. Plants can now be obtained from www. dolcarevolucio.cat .

13.Perella/*Shiso*. Annual. An interesting purple-leafed plant. Can leave to grow to 50cm high or trim to keep neat. Leaves can be used in salads or in infusions. Anti-allergy and anti-inflammatory properties. Traditionally used in Japanese raw fish Shiso dishes to help prevent stomach aches from contaminated fish. Let a couple of branches go to seed for the next year. Semi-shade.

Recently found a seed pack that makes growing from seed very practical without having to buy a large packet of seeds, pots, compost etc. (See section 9.5 D). Also available for a good number of other herbs.

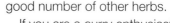

If you are a curry enthusiast it's possible to grow your own ingredients. The photograph shows a friend's Andalusian roof-top curry garden in January with a large curry tree with spicy leaves, lemon grass, chillies, tumeric, bay and garlic. In the summer annual coriander and other herbs are grown alongside the productive orange and lemon trees.

7.5 Some Special Herb Care Needs

1. Annual herbs can be mostly killed off by under-watering but also by getting them waterlogged. If you find you have problems with rotting, water less and spray the soil and young stems with propolis.

2. Perennials can be mostly killed by over-watering and allowing the foliage to become to large for the size of the root ball. So transplant into a bigger pot when you buy them and trim often, but not until they are bare, to stimulate young growth, but keep foliage ball and root ball balanced. Don't use pots less then 15 to 20cm diameter. Naturally they can also be killed by long periods of no watering.

3. Although many herbs survive well on Mediterranean mountainsides, they put down very deep roots to find the last drop of summer moisture and the deep roots enable frost-burnt plants to recover. This cannot happen in containers so ensure there is sufficient residual moisture between waterings while avoiding waterlogging and fast drainage. Your compost mix is therefore important. A poor soil with little nutrient content will result in stressed and diseased plants. We suggest the following mix for both the annuals and perennials to use when transplanting to larger containers — an enriched peat-based compost with 10 per cent sand or vermiculite added. We find that some crushed palm fibre-based composts dry out too fast.

4. When growing from seeds first sow in a 15cm pot of vermiculite. When 4cm high with two to four leaves, prick out with a flat tooth pick and slide into a 2cm-deep hole made with a pencil in a 10cm pot of the above compost. When established, re-pot into a 15 to 20cm pot or part of an equivalent area of a window box.

5. If your pots dry out too fast in the sun, relocate to the semi-shade but ensure they still get four hours of morning or evening sun in the summer. They don't like full shade all day.

6. If you find it difficult to keep some perennial herbs going throughout the year, decide to buy new plants each spring and regard them as annuals. They are not expensive.

7.6 When and How to Harvest and Store Herbs

Cut as often as the plants will stand without dying – always leave some new green growth to keep the process of photosynthesis going. This is the process that plants use to synthesis natural nutrients from carbon dioxide from the air and moisture. A by-product is chlorophyll that greens plants.

If not cut continuously, herbs such as rocket, parsley, basil and coriander easily go to seed so cut off flower buds and flowers to achieve continuous new growth and a longer harvesting period.

If you cannot keep up with the plants' growth, look up some more recipes that use herbs, start to drink more herb infusions and cut and dry what still can't be used. If you cut long stems, they can be tied into a bunch and hung from the cut stem end in a dry warm spot on the terrace. You leave them hanging and use as required, or break off the leaves and store in an airtight jar, or freeze some in the ice tray and add the herby cubes to soups etc.

A couple of bunches of dried herbs hanging from the ceiling of a covered terrace will sometimes attract insect-catching geckoes. Useful — and fun to watch harmless surviving wildlife in the urban environment.

7.7 Ten Beneficial Herb Infusions From Your Apartment Terrace

1. Mint – useful as a digestive and to relieve a hangover. Since there are many types of mint you can vary the delicate flavours. Good alternative to tea and coffee.

2. Lemon verbena – is a medium-sized shrub whose leaves and flowers can be trimmed from the end of branches to prepare a particularly refreshing drink especially on a hot afternoon. A good alternative for delicate teas for calming nerves. Good cold with ice.

3. Rosemary – infusions give an energy and memory boost. Both useful when we were writing this book. We also chew the leaves to release the oil when feeling weary on long walks...

4. Sage – infusions act as an antiseptic especially for teeth and gums.

5. Parsley – infusions of special benefit to ladies who suffer from cystitis. Also a diuretic.

6. Rue – we find that infusions speed recovery from sprains and strains incurred mountain walking and playing tennis

7. Garlic – an infusion can be sprayed on geraniums and other plants to deter insects.

8. Thyme – an infusion is a long-standing antiseptic and decongestant.

9. Basil – with fresh lemon slices, grated or sliced ginger plus black pepper is our potent infusion should we feel signs of a cold.

10. Stevia – an infusion of this natural sweetener, which is said to be healthier than sugar and artificial sweeteners, has been found to be beneficial by diabetics. A fresh or ground leaf can be added to any infusion as a sweetener.

So herbs are useful for their leaf and flower colours, their aromas, cooking and health. Make sure you have a few varieties.

Container -grown Fruit

A good number of fruits can be grown in containers on apartment windowsills, balconies and terraces. There will not be orchard-size harvests but the ecologically grown fruit can be harvested when at their best as a welcome addition to your diet. And the annual blossoms and bright-coloured fruit can be attractive additions to the effects achieved with other plants.

8.1 Some Good Reasons For Growing Fruit

There are many good reasons why everyone with a property in Spain, including an apartment, should ensure that at least a lemon tree or grapevine is among other plants being grown.

• You will be able to eat some of your favourite fruits at their best – raw, juiced, in salads or in cooked dishes.

• Fruit trees can be attractive as many have pleasing foliage, many being evergreen. Blossom and fruits are generally brightly coloured when ripening. Fruit trees are among the first spring-flowering trees and the perfume of citrus tree blossom is heavy and uplifting.

• Not much space is required. For instance, a perpetual lunar lemon can be fitted into the corner of any terrace; a grapevine can be grown in a 40-50cm tub and trained on a wall or trellis; a peach tree can be grown in a similar sized tub and pruned into a 40-50cm columnar shape or trained into a fan shape on a wall or trellis; mandarin trees could be located on either side of the doorway of a balcony; some 30 strawberry plants can be planted in the holes of a typical 60cm-high strawberry barrel which only takes up the space of an A3 sheet of paper; a line/mini hedge of trimmed dwarf pomegranate could be grown in a window box or trough; and mandarin trees in a trough or line of tubs can be trimmed into a thick fruiting hedge/windbreak.

• It is easy to grow fruit trees and plants ecologically so that you know there will be no residual orchard or packing station chemicals on the skins.

• You will have two or three of the daily fruit intake recommended by health authorities growing on your very own balcony or terrace.

• If you have a number of terraces and one is little used, you could convert it into a mini orchard with columnar bastion fruit trees as close as only 75cm apart. In containers the

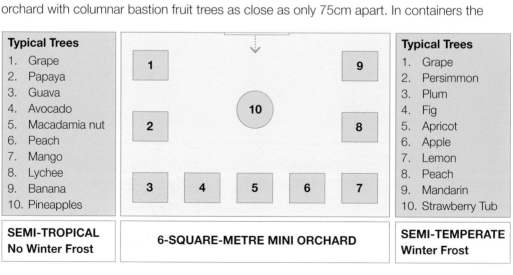

Typical Trees	6-SQUARE-METRE MINI ORCHARD	Typical Trees
1. Grape		1. Grape
2. Papaya		2. Persimmon
3. Guava		3. Plum
4. Avocado		4. Fig
5. Macadamia nut		5. Apricot
6. Peach		6. Apple
7. Mango		7. Lemon
8. Lychee		8. Peach
9. Banana		9. Mandarin
10. Pineapples		10. Strawberry Tub
SEMI-TROPICAL **No Winter Frost**	**6-SQUARE-METRE MINI ORCHARD**	**SEMI-TEMPERATE** **Winter Frost**

roots will not be competing for moisture and nutrients as they would be in an orchard where trees are planted five metres apart. The plan is for a six-square-metre terrace or the end of a long narrow terrace. All trees are in 40cm-wide, 60cm-deep tubs and the grapevines in 30 x 60cm troughs.

- It's an interesting pastime for those whose gardening is restricted to apartment terraces and balconies.

These benefits are unquestionable so why not start this week. But before you plant a mini orchard do check the weight-bearing load of your balcony and terrace.

8.2 What Should You Grow?

Most readers will have limited space so it makes most sense to grow those fruits that:

a. Are among the easiest to grow in containers

b. Can be pruned to be of a convenient size for balconies and small and medium-sized terraces. Naturally they can all be pruned less if planted in larger containers and allowed to grow bigger for large terraces including those of penthouses.

c. You like.

d. Are suitable for your microclimate

e. Have a long harvesting time to maximise the productivity of your available space

f. Can take up little space even when mature.

▲ Dwarf fruit trees

g. Can be purchased in dwarf varieties. Alternatively, a regular variety's size can be successfully controlled by growing in a container to restrict the growth of the root ball and by pruning.

h. Are available in seed form. See www.jungleseeds.co.uk for starters. Will take time until you have crops but it's an interesting challenge.

Based on these criteria we suggest that you start with fruits from the two selections that follow. The first is of fruits suitable for areas that never experience frosts and the second for areas that definitely have frosts most years. A baker's dozen of each are given. We have including things for the beginner as well as the experienced and indicate the ease of growing.

Fruits for locations that never experience frosts

Lemon – Easy – Evergreen. Preferable buy a perpetual flowering and fruiting varieties so that there will be lemons to harvest each month of the year. Lunar, Cuatro estaciones and Eureka are suitable varieties. Also stands up to frosts.

Lime – Moderately easy – Evergreen. Buy a young plant.

Mandarin – Easy – Evergreen. Before buying decide whether you want an early midseason or late season variety. Stands up to frosts.

Avocado – Moderately easy – Evergreen. Buy plant or grow from seed if patient. Best on larger terrace. Reasonably frost-resistant.

Guava – Moderately easy – Evergreen. Buy a plant or seeds from www.jungleseeds.co.uk.

Mango – Moderately easy – Evergreen. Buy a plant.

Grape – Moderately easy – Deciduous. Buy a plant and train up a wall or over an arbour. Frost-resistant.

Passion fruit – Easy. Buy a plant or grow from seed. Several edible varieties available from www.chilteernseeds.co.uk and www.jungleseeds.co.uk. Some frost-resistant.

Paraquaya – Moderately easy – Deciduous. Wonderful taste when ripe – somewhere between a peach and a nectarine. Buy a plant and train as a fan on wall or trellis screen.

Banana – Moderately difficult – Evergreen. Plants can be purchased and also grown from seed. Purchased ones tend to be of a large growing variety most suited for large terraces but seeds for a wide range of smaller varieties can be found in the seed catalogues of www.chilternseeds.co.uk and www.jungleseeds.co.uk.

Papaya – Moderately difficult – Semi-evergreen. Buy a plant. Seeds germinate easily but they tend to rot at the seedling stage. But if you are green-fingered have a go.

Star fruit – Moderately difficult. You may find a plant or grow one from the seeds from a fruit.

Pineapple – Difficult. Grown from the top of a pineapple. Cut top off, cut off half the leaves, dry the end, plant in a rich compost mix in a 10cm pot and just keep damp. Re-pot into a larger pot after a year and with luck you may harvest a pineapple in the second year. Edible pineapple plants are also occasionally seen in garden centres.

It will take several years before you have good harvests of some of the above, but in the meantime their foliages are interesting and give shade and privacy.

Knowing that you will only have a limited space and recognising the tremendous differences between the hottest terraces of the Andalusia coastline and the coolest in Valencia and Cataluña, we left out figs and peaches from the above list but you could add them. They are in the list below.

Fruits for areas that can expect to experience pockets of frost most years

Kumquat – Easy – Most frost-resistant citrus. Buy well-shaped youngish tree. May well fruit first year but suggest you remove when young the first year to build up tree.

Tangerine or mandarin– Moderately easy. Buy well shaped young tree. Quite possibly three or four years before good fruiting. More frost-resistant than oranges or grapefruit.

Lemon – Moderately easy. Buy well shaped young plant. Quite possible three or four years before good fruiting. Again more frost-resistant than oranges.

Peach – Easy. Best to buy early eating versus later cooking variety. Good crops likely in second year.

Apple – Easy. Buy an early variety. Good crops possible in second year.

Persimmon – Easy. Buy young tree of Sharon variety that is less astringent. Fruits probable in second year.

Pear – Moderately easy. Buy tree. Tends to have more pest problems that other fruits.

Plum – Moderately easy. Buy tree – Red and yellow varieties available

Fig – Moderately easy. Early and late fruiting varieties and black or green fruits available.

Grape – Moderately easy. A climber. Buy a vine, black, pink and white varieties available. Train on wall, on a frame or over an arbour.

Pomegranate – Moderately easy/easiest with miniature varieties. Buy a tree. Waxy bright orange flowers. May be five years before fruit.

Strawberries – Easy. Buy plants or grow from seed if you want the small sweetest alpine strawberries. Grow in a strawberry barrel window box or larger trough.

Olives – Moderately easy. Interesting foliage. Gives a Mediterranean feel. Can be pruned hard. May take some years to fruit then eventually an abundance. Best on larger terraces.

These are selected from the 70 fruits described as suitable for the various regions of the Mediterranean area – towards hot sub tropical and towards cooler temperate – in our earlier book *Growing Healthy Fruits in Spain*.

We have not included our favourite fruit of all, raspberries, for only on a large terrace could one afford the space for 20 or more plants to make it worthwhile. Also they would need summer shading.

Naturally, before making your final decisions about what to plant on your balconies or terraces, you will want to understand when each of the selected fruits should be planted, pruned and fed, and when the trees will flower and have fruits ready for harvesting. This combined list is in alphabetical order to help you trace the fruits.

NAME OF FRUIT TREE English, Spanish and *botanical names*	Best time to plant	Frost resis- tance	Drought resis- tance	Pruning time	Typical blossom time	Typical harvest time
APPLE Manzano *Malus communis*	Late autumn/ winter	High	Medium	Winter	March/ April	August to October
AVOCADO Aguacate *Persia gratisoima*	Spring	Mod	Medium	Spring	Jan/ March	October to June
BANANA Platanera *Musa paradisiaca*	Early summer	Low	Low	When dead leaves	April/ July	Sept to March
FIG Higuera *Ficus carica*	Late autumn/ winter	High	High	Winter	No visible flowers	July to October
GRAPEVINE Vid *Vitis vinifera*	Late Winter/ Spring	High	High	Winter/ Spring	April/ May	July to October
GUAVA Guayaba *Psidium quajava*	Spring	Low	Medium	Winter	April/ May	July/ August
KIWINI Kiwinin *Actinidia arguta*	Spring	Medium/ high	Low/ medium	Winter	May/ June	Aug/Oct
KUMQUAT Naranja china *Citrus fortunella margarita*	Spring	High	Medium	March	March/ April	Dec/ March

NAME OF FRUIT TREE English, Spanish and *botanical names*	Best time to plant	Frost resis-tance	Drought resis-tance	Pruning time	Typical blossom time	Typical harvest time
LEMON Limón *Citrus limon*	Spring	Mod	Medium	March	Perpetual *	Perpetual *
LIME Lima *Citrus aurantifolia*	Spring	Low	Medium	March	March/ April	October/ Nov.
MANDARIN Mandarina *Citrus pecticulata*	Spring	Mod	Medium	March	March/ April	Nov. to May**
MANGO Mango *Mangifera indica*	Spring	Low	Medium	Spring	April/ June	August/ Sept.
PAPAYA Papaya *Carica papaya*	Late spring	Low	Low	Winter	March/ June	June/ August
PARAGUAYA Paraguaya *Prunus persica var. platycarpa*	Late autumn/ winter	Low	Medium	Winter	April/ May	July/ August
PASSION FRUIT Pasionaria *Passiflora edulis*	Spring	Mod	Medium/ high	Winter	April to October	June to October
PEACH Melocotonero *Prunus perica*	Late autumn/ winter	High	Medium	Winter	March/ May **	June/ Sept. **
PEAR Peral *Pyrus*	Late autumn/ winter	High	Medium	Winter/ Summer	March/ April	June/ Nov. **
PERSIMMON Caqui *Diesphros kaki.*	Late autumn / winter	High	Medium	Winter	April/ May	Sept./ Dec
PINEAPPLE Piña *Ananas comosus*	Autumn	Low	Low	None	Summer	Autumn

NAME OF FRUIT TREE English, Spanish and *botanical names*	Best time to plant	Frost resistance	Drought resistance	Pruning time	Typical blossom time	Typical harvest time
PLUM Ciruela *Prunus sativa*	Late autumn/ winter	High	Medium	Winter	March/ April	June/ July
POMEGRANATE Granado *Punica granatum*	Late autumn/ winter	High	High	Winter	May	October/ February
STAR FRUIT Carambola *Averrhoa carambola*	Spring	Low	Low	Spring	April/May And Sept/Oct	Aug/Sept and Dec/Feb
STRAWBERRY (cultivated) Fresón *Frageria aranassa*	Autumn to Spring	High	Medium	Winter	March to October	March to October
ALPINE STRAWBERRY Fresa *Fragaria vesca*	Autumn or Spring	High	Medium	Winter	March to October	March to October
TANGERINE Tangerina *Citrus tangerina*	Spring	Medium/ High	Medium	Spring	March to April	Nov. to January

Notes: *We recommend you plant a perpetual variety such as Lunar, Cuatro Estaciones or Eureka.
**Dependent on varieties. Melons are not mentioned in the table as they take up a lot of space. However, if you have a large terrace and happen to eat a really tasty canteloupe melon, keep the seeds and have a go!

8.3 Selection Of Containers

SIZE

The diameter and depth need to be sufficient to allow:

- a widening root ball to grow without becoming root-bound for three to five years,
- roots to grow downwards and not to and around the circumference of the container wall
- sufficient compost to be contained to hold a good reservoir of moisture, especially during periods of hot weather.

Typical sizes are as follows:

What is to be planted?	Suggested minimum size of container:		
	Depth cms	Width or diameter cms	Volume litres compost
A lemon tree	40	40	35
A grapevine	50	40 or 50	80
Strawberries in			
a. barrel	30	30	20
b. trough	20	60 x 40	50
Olive tree for penthouse terrace	80	100	500

WATERING AND PREVENTION OF MOISTURE LOSSES

Typical watering needs for a fruit tree in a 40cm-high, 40cm-wide tub will be five litres every two days in the middle of summer and five litres a week in the winter.

It is important that roots do not dry out as roots are not forgiving. So ensure your containers are not porous. If you want to use terracotta containers, paint them inside with a waterproofing paint and allow it to dry before filling with compost. Also place pot trays under containers to retain moisture and prevent staining tiles.

AESTHETICS

Chose good-looking ceramic or terracotta substitute plastic pots or tubs. Terracotta, green or wood coloured containers match fruit trees and plants well. Suggest you avoid fussier colours and designs, which, in our view, go better with flowers.

8.4 Buying Fruit Plants, Bushes and Trees

Think about your needs before touring garden centres. If tempted to buy something extra, ask yourself whether you will have room for more or should you substitute it for something else.

It is wise to check each plant or tree for the following before buying:

• Healthy growth. No obvious signs that they have been allowed to dry out.

• A good root ball in relation to the size of the foliage of the plant you intend to buy. If possible, lift an example out of the pot and loosen the soil to check.

• The root ball is not seriously root-bound and a strong central corkscrew not yet well developed or hardened, which would make it difficult to spread the roots out before planting. Mature corkscrew roots are one of the main reasons fruit trees become stunted and die back after a few years.

• No obvious sign of pests.

• No broken or seriously misshapen branches.

• A label clearly indicating what you are buying. Otherwise it is very easy for types and varieties to become mixed up at the nursery and on your journey home.

When buying fruit trees, ask the nursery if they have any fruit trees grafted to dwarf rooting stock which will keep the trees naturally small. If not, chose young trees with branches or signs of buds all the way up the trunk that you will be able to prune and train into a columnar bastion shaped tree which will take up less space than a bush-shaped tree. Fan trees need to be trained on a wall or length of trellis and an umbrella-shaped tree will give summer shade on an open terrace and penthouse roof.

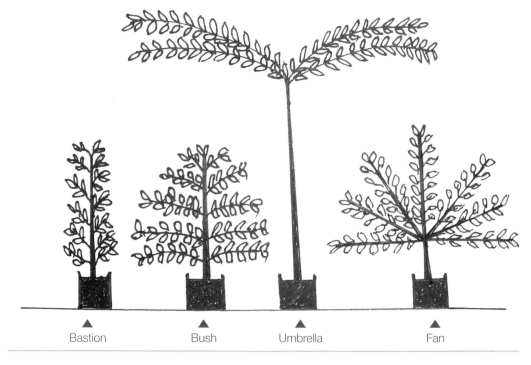

| Bastion | Bush | Umbrella | Fan |

In general, it's wise to plant deciduous trees and bushes during the autumn and early winter to allow the roots to settle in and start to grow strongly before the first summer. In areas definitely not affected by air frosts evergreen trees are best purchased and planted in late winter. In other areas in early spring after the risk of serious frost is past.

If you buy a tree with fruit on it, remove the fruit. This allows the tree to concentrate on forming a strong spreading-root ball and foliage before having to concentrate on forming fruit.

8.5 Planting Your Plants and Trees

How well you plant your fruit trees and plants is fundamental to their success.
The main things to avoid are:

- Not preparing a good compost mix .
- Using too small a container.
- Not separating out and spreading out the roots when placing in the compost. If you don't the intertwined roots will corkscrew and eventually strangle the tree.
- Not firming the compost as the container is filled and around plants and trees when planted.
- Not ensuring there is a drainage hole at the bottom of the container to prevent waterlogging. Two centimetres of broken pots or crockery at the bottom of the pot above the drainage hole/s can help with drainage.
- Adding chemical fertilisers when planting or soon after. This can burn young roots especially with citrus fruits.

GUIDELINES FOR PLANTING

1. Bags of flowering plant compost are unlikely to provide the necessary rich, loamy, growing medium full of natural essential nutrients and a balance of water retention and free draining properties. We therefore recommend that you make up one of the following mixes.

   a. If you have access to some garden soil, make up a 2:1:1 mix of soil, bagged peat-based compost from the garden centre and bagged animal manure or worm compost.

   b. If you cannot obtain garden soil, substitute turf-based compost which has a high soil content in the above mix.

   c. Strawberries like acidic soil so ensure you use a compost compounded for acid-loving plants in the above mixes.

   d. Add five per cent of coarse sand to each of the mixes to help drainage.

   e. Water retention can be increased by adding about five grams of TerraCottem soil-improving gel to each litre of compost mix. That is about a teaspoonful. This will be particularly beneficial during the summer months.

A builders'/gardeners' large plastic bucket is good for doing the mixing up.

2. Place two centimetres of broken pots crockery or small stones above the drainage holes.

3. For trees measure the depth of the pot or plastic sleeve in which you purchased the fruit tree and fill the chosen container with compost, firming as you proceed, until the distance to the top of the container is the depth measurement you took plus five centimetres. Separate instructions for planting strawberries will be given latter.

4. Remove the tree from the pot and separate the roots from the soil and untwine them. Many will have started to be root-bound and, especially if grown in narrow tubes, to develop a corkscrew of roots rather than an open umbrella of roots as on a bare rooted tree grown in open ground.

5. Spread the roots as evenly as possible on top of the compost and then fill in firming the compost as you go.

6. Water the compost well and keep the lowest roots damp. Recognise that roots can dry out and die as easily from the bottom as from the top.

7. If planting climbers or trees you plan to prune as fans place the container in front of a wall or trellis and tie in.

PLANTING STRAWBERRIES

1. Fill the strawberry barrel with the compost mix to the level of the first level of planting holes.

2. Take a plant out of the plant pot you purchased in and remove sufficient compost to be able to push the roots through a planting hole.

3. Spread the roots and cover with and firm the compost.

4. Repeat the process until all planting holes are planted and top up with compost to within 5cm of the top of the barrel.

5. To minimise the evaporation of moisture if planting strawberries in a raised bed, planting table, window box or trough, mulch the plants with a layer of black plastic sheeting by cutting a hole in the sheet and threading the planted strawberry plant through the hole. Finally, cover with a little compost to hold it down and for neatness.

6. Water the new plants well.

8.6 Watering Guidelines

Keep the compost mix just damp at al times down to the level of the deepest roots. Watering every two days will probably be required during hot weather while once a week may suffice during spells of cooler winter weather. If you are always at home, a few containers can be easily watered with a watering can or terrace hose if installed.

With fruit trees and bushes in tubs it helps to keep the compost level 5cm below the rim and flood the tub up to the rim when watering. To help water a strawberry barrel push lengths of 3 or 4cm-diameter plastic tubing into the compost. One almost to the bottom of the barrel, one to two-thirds down and a third to a third of the depth. If you water through these and on the surface, all the root balls should remain damp. Such tubes are also useful for watering fruit trees and bushes.

If you are likely to be away during the year or regularly forgetful or lazy in respect of watering, we recommend that you install a mini drip system. You can easy make one up and DIY kits for small systems are sometimes available. Ask your local horticultural shop to look them up their catalogues.

It helps if one mixes 50 grams of TerraCottem (www.terravida.com) soil improvement gel per 10 litres of compost mix. This product helps improve the water-holding capacity of the compost. There will then be an emergency moisture reserve should you forget to water for a few days or if the timer battery on a watering system stops and goes unnoticed for a few days. Often the latter is because the battery is dead, so change it every three months as a safeguard.

Container-grown fruit trees benefit from a water mist spray from a small hand-held sprayer in the evening during hot summer months.

8.7 Feeding Guidelines

If you prepared a rich compost mix as suggested in Section 8.5, you will not need to give the trees a supplementary feed for a year.

Then use a general balanced ecological fertiliser at the end of the first winter and the following year onwards switch to fertiliser with a higher potassium content to stimulate flowers and fruits. If you have a large number of fruits formed, another feed in late spring can be beneficial. We prefer to use a dilute strength liquid feed versus a strong granular feed. Should the foliage suffer from frost, a cold wind or your forgetting to water, give the leaves a dilute nitrogen foliar feed.

8.8 What Pruning Will Be Required?

When growing fruit trees in containers the main purposes of pruning will be as follows:

• To develop a balanced and pleasing shaped tree. When you first purchase your tree we suggest you don't prune for the first year or two until you see which are the strongest branches and what natural shape develops once the tree becomes settled in the container. Except when wanting to grow a columnar tree, when it is necessary to cut off the top 10 to 20cm and trim back the longest branches to stimulate new branches sprouting lower down the trunk. The garden centre will normally do this for you if you ask.

• To reduce the strain on the root system if a tree is growing too large for the container, unless you have space to re-pot into a larger container.

The signs are of the tree starting to look unhealthy after a few years and all of a sudden poorer crops. It's better to decide on the size of container and eventual tree at the beginning.

- To train trees into fan shapes trained on a trellis frame or wall.
- Cut out the previous year's growth as with grape and kiwini vines.
- Thin out fruits on vines and trees as they mature to stimulate larger fruits.
- Trimming non-fruiting branches to stimulate fruiting side shoots.
- Remove runners on strawberry plants each winter. These can be potted up to grow replacement or additional plants. Strawberry plants are best changed every three years.
- Removing diseased growth.

The best time for pruning is indicated in the table in Section 8.2. If you want to know more about pruning in Spain refer to *Growing Healthy Fruit in Spain.*

8.9 Watching Out For Problems

Most pests and diseases are caused by under and over-watering, so take care in this respect. Spray trees and plants preventively each month against various moths flies and other insects with Neem oil (5cc in a litre of water) or another ecological general insecticide and watch out for any problems. If you see signs of accumulations of insects or browning of leaves or lumps of a honey-like substance on the trunks or branches, refer to section 10.2 looking at the photographs or reading the description of possible problems to identify your problem. Then read and act on the advice given.

8.10 Knowing When and How To Harvest

Aim to harvest fruit when it is at its best according to taste, texture, aroma and colour. The only sure way of knowing when this occurs is to try a fruit and eat it off the tree or cut it up on a plate and let several members of the family try it. Remove all fruits from trees or plants by gently holding the fruit and turning it.

If the fruit is ripe it will loosen and come off immediately. If it resists strongly, leave fruit on the tree for a few more days before trying again. If you have never grown your own fruit before or been to a PYO orchard you may be in for a pleasant surprise.

8.11 What To Do With Your Harvests

You will hopefully be harvesting from your fruit trees when the fruit is at its best so the best thing is to eat directly from the trees and plants. Second best is storing a few days' supply in the chill drawer of your refrigerator, except for strawberries that need eating the day they are harvested. Fruit not eaten immediately, especially if you have a glut, can be frozen or dried or made into marmelade jam or chutney.

Container-grown vegetables

More and more apartment-dwellers in Spain and other areas with a Mediterranean climate are growing fresh, healthy, seasonal vegetables on their terraces, balconies and windowsills. We explain why you should consider doing likewise and how it can be done most easily in very small spaces.

9.1 Seeing is Believing

The series of photographs on the opposite and next page illustrate what others have already done to grow vegetables successfully on a micro and mini scale. It is not difficult and can be an interesting and healthy activity. As you will see, it is possible to dedicate entire small terraces to producing daily, fresh, ecological vegetables. But most people just add it to the growing of flowers herbs and perhaps one or two fruit trees. You will have seen that the plan for the dream penthouse terrace in Section 3.5 included many of the proven ideas described in the various sections of Part Nine. One of the greatest benefits is being able to pick an amazing mix of fresh salad leaves every day of the year.

A. MICRO-SCALE – OR A4 VEGGIE-GROWING

Micro scale vegetable-growing involves only using the space equivalent to one or two A4 sheets of paper (i.e. only one square foot). This can be amazingly productive, especially in Mediterranean climate locations which enjoy two springs – spring and autumn – as well as in many cases a mild winter for over-wintering plants. The photographs on the next three pages illustrate eight practical ways of micro scale production.

1. Various vegetables in pots

Many vegetables can be grown in individual medium-sized pots. Photograph One shows a group of planted-up pots. Some of the easiest vegetables to start with include:

- A purchased tomato pepper or aubergine plant.
- Young garlic by breaking up a garlic bulb and planting the individual cloves to grow the young shoots for salad omelettes and adding mild flavour to cooked dishes.
- Chives from seed or by buying a plant or two.
- Carrots that have one of the lowest germinating temperatures.
- Peas that can hang over the pot or be supported on canes.

2. Cut-and-come-again lettuces in plastic storage box

The second photograph shows cut-and-come-again lettuce leaves grown in an inexpensive small plastic storage box. The first leaves were cut and eaten only four weeks after planting the seeds and harvesting continued for two months. Two weeks before this a second box was started for continuity. In similar boxes radishes baby carrots and cherry tomatoes could also be grown and the boxes could be placed as a square block or a line.

3. Short-length window boxes

The window boxes in this photograph really took up no space. The window boxes hanging from the security bars of a windowsill supported on rope with cane supports underneath each. The top box had been just recently planted with three trailing tomato plants which were protected by three cut-off five-litre water bottles as nights were still chilly. The next box down was planted with cut-and-come-again oriental salad leaves, the third with basil chives parsley for adding to salads and the lowest with quickly maturing radishes. Diverse crops for interesting salads. No not enormous crops but it illustrates what can be done with a little creativity. The concept could have been expanded to cover an entire wall on a small open terrace or even a balcony.

4. Tomatoes without losing your petunias

For fun we experimented with improving the productivity of apartment window boxes for photograph four. We drilled two small holes in the base of a self-watering window box, threaded two pieces of 5mm irrigation tubing through the holes and sealed where the tubes entered and exited the plastic, then carefully threaded the roots of two young tomato plants upwards through the bottom. The window box was then filled with compost and petunias were planted on the top.

5. Recycled plastic water bottles

All sizes of empty water and soft drink plastic bottles with the tops cut off can be usefully recycled: 500ml bottles can be used to grow garlic and onions; 1.5 litre bottles leeks and parsnips; and 5 and 7-litre bottles as alternatives for pots and tubs for sowing seeds, planting plantlets for many types of vegetables. Ninety per cent of the tops of the larger bottles can be cut off and left with a hinge so that they can be used as cloches in early spring until the weather warms up and young plants are hardened off.

6. Potato towers or barrels

For many years potatoes were frequently grown in large pots or small plastic dustbins but today easier-to-use proprietary potato towers (as illustrated) are sold by several mail order catalogues – see page 216. The main advantages are that their base is less than one square foot and the bottom half of some can be slid upwards to remove new potatoes as they form.

7. Autumn wild mushrooms in a bag

The next photograph shows a typical crop from a purchased plastic sack of fertilised, dampened straw which has been impregnated with the spawn of oyster mushrooms. A number of varieties of wild mushrooms and also cultivated button mushrooms can be grown this way. Easy to fit into a corner of a north-facing terrace as the temperatures drop in the autumn. Three crops between November and February is a normal harvest.

8. Sprouting seeds in tray

The last photograph in the series shows sprouting seeds being grown in inexpensive plastic trays and a more expensive automatic watering sprouter. As explained in Section 9.3, at least 20 different types of seed can be easily sprouted on a terrace or in the kitchen when the terrace is too hot. Open trays can be protected from insects by covering them with a domed mesh food cover.

A sprouter can turn a few grams of seeds into a kilo of sprouted seeds in a week. Most families would not to like to consume only those vegetables and not that much in a week, but it highlights just what can be done to live more healthily without a large vegetable garden and without ever getting your hands dirty with compost.

Micro vegetables can also be grown in shallow trays but this time in shallow compost. Seeds such as mustard and cress and broccoli are sown on the surface and then lightly covered with fine compost. They are then watered and placed in a warm semi-shaded place to germinate and grow. The crop is harvested when there are two to six small leaves on each seedling by cutting them off just above the compost.

B. MINI-SCALE – ONE SQUARE METRE VEGGIE-GROWING

Lets move up a scale to mini vegetable growing in less than one square metre of terrace or balcony space. The possibilities include: a very productive group of small and large pots, raised beds and growing table allotments, a disused bath and grow bags.

9. A group of pots

The small pots at the front are part of a collection of herbs. In the three large 60/70cm-diameter plastic pots more than a dozen different vegetables were growing in the containers at the time. In one the surface vegetables could be harvested up to November and, when cleared to prepare to re-sow, a dozen sizeable sweet potatoes were harvested from the bottom layers of compost. They had grown below the level of the roots of the other vegetables and the leafy stems were trailed down the side of the plastic pot and down the side of the terrace where they looked decorative and caused no mess for anyone below. By the way the area taken up on a medium-sized terrace was only just over a square metre!

10. A raised bed

A wood surround for raised beds up to a meter square are easily made by yourself or a local carpenter. Wood, plastic and woven plastic cloth ones can be found in Internet garden supply and seed catalogues. See page 216. The sides are normally 20 to 30cm high to give the depth of seed required for most vegetable plants. Deeper-rooted

ones like globe artichoke, potatoes and parsnips can be grown in medium or large-sized pots or barrels. If you just have wooden sides without a base, a strong black lining fixed to the top of the sides will stop moisture seeping into the tiles and compost seeping out around the raised bed. Will fit at the end of any terrace but you need to kneel down to work on it. They are therefore more convenient and comfortable with a solid wooden base and 30cm legs or even longer legs converted into a growing table.

11. A growing table

The table shown is made of galvanised steel and that in Section C from marine ply lined with plastic. Both were made by local tradesmen. The 80cm legs have casters and therefore one can move the table around and work on it while standing up or sitting on a stool. Shorter legs were supplied to drop the table down to 30cm to use as a raised bed that could be worked by children kneeling down. The unit was made up inexpensively by our local carpenter, but commercially produced versions are now available in wood and aluminium and galvanised steel – see page 216 for addresses.

Naturally any size can be constructed by a handy man but the width needs to be a maximum of 80cm for working from one side and 150cm when working from two sides. The compost depth is normally 20cm deep so that most vegetables can be grown.

12. An old bath

If you have just had the bathroom modernised and you are not too bothered by aesthetics, follow the example in the bath photograph. Initially it yielded two and a half kilos of rice and then proved to be an excellent mini raised bed for growing carrots, mini lettuces and broccoli. In effect the bath was used as a large plastic trough. You can buy troughs with built-in water reservoirs in many garden centres.

13. Grow bags

Grow bags are useful for both fruit and leaf vegetables. They can be lined up along railings or walls, placed on top of tables and sideboards or used as a block like a raised bed. Floragard now market two grow bags. A red one with compost suitable for summer tomatoes peppers and aubergines, or winter peas and broad beans. A green one suitable for leaf vegetables such as lettuces, Swiss chard and mini cabbages and flower vegetables such as cauliflowers and broccoli.

C. MACRO-SCALE – TWO METRES PLUS

If you are keen to expand your efforts, you can dedicate several square metres of a terrace, large or small, covered or open, to vegetable growing. The terrace shown (unfortunately not yet in full production) is 1.5 by 2.5 metres and faces south-east. It incorporates several of the types of containers previously discussed.

The terrace was inspired by a rooftop vegetable plot we discovered in a village in

Andalusia with a marvellous view of Gibraltar and the mountains of Morocco and a small terrace several floors up in an apartment block in the centre of Valencia.

What a good idea for a group of students sharing a flat and determined to eat better and be partially self-sufficient. The photograph on page 43 showing a small terrace surrounded by succulents could equally be a vegetable terrace.

Another alternative for large open terraces is a "Ten-tub veggie plot", which we launched in our book *Growing Healthy Vegetables in Spain*. As illustrated, you need 10 plastic pots 60 to 10cm in diameter. To minimise the space required they are best positioned in two rows as shown. One can walk between and reach across the pots to work. The plan also shows a water tank at one end with a small submerged solar pump for an irrigation system and a mini greenhouse for raising seedlings. In the coming years many more terraces are likely to be dedicated to growing vegetables as the traditional huertos, or smallholdings/allotments, surrounding villages and cities are abandoned because of low prices for the growers and a renewed demand for land for the construction of buildings and transport networks.

The 10-Tub Concept

9.2 Why Not Do the Same?

You have seen what is possible so why not do something similar? We summarise some of the main reasons below.

1. Increasingly health authorities in Spain and worldwide are exhorting us to eat more vegetables, specifically at least five to nine portions of fruit and vegetables a day, with vegetables predominating.

2. It is becoming more and more difficult to purchase really fresh vegetables when at their best. That requires them to be harvested daily for consumption the same day. Unfortunately there has been a decline in the local production of vegetables as previously worked agricultural land has been built on or abandoned as middle-aged and elderly agriculturalists cannot obtain prices that cover their costs and the next generations expect a better standard of living.

▲ Mini vegetable seeds from several suppliers

3. It's not difficult and can be a fascinating and satisfying hobby. The better seed merchants now sell seeds of specially-bred mini varieties of vegetables. These can be grown closer together than larger varieties so need less space and create less waste and always fresher vegetables as a large lettuce does not need to be eaten over several days by a single family.

4. If children live in your apartment, involving them in the growing of salad vegetables for their lunch-time rolls and other meals can encourage them to understand what vegetables are, where they come from and that it's fun to grow them.

5. Even if you only grow vegetables on a mini scale you can ensure that they are grown ecologically and reduce the risk of consuming residual chemical insecticides and fungicides and chemicals intended to enhance shelf life.

6. The Mediterranean climate ensures two springs, spring and autumn, so there are much longer natural growing periods than in northern Europe. Further, your sheltered terrace – unless a penthouse swept by freezing blasts from ski resort areas – will rarely be affected by frosts so if facing south tomatoes can even be grown throughout the year in warmer areas.

7. You are not only able to harvest fresh vegetables daily but to do so when the vegetables are at their best in terms of taste, aroma, texture and appearance.

8. You can reduce the time and money travelling to shops.

9. You will be doing something positive about your daily wellness if you concentrate on growing the vegetables with health benefits.

10. Growing vegetables on your terrace requires no prior experience or specialist tools.

11. Your outlay can be minimal if recycled containers are used.

12. The whole family can be involved.

9.3 What Can Be Grown For Health?

We are often asked at talks what vegetables we would grow if we had restricted growing space and everything had to be grown in containers of one sort or another.
Our reply is always: "Those that can contribute most to our continuing good health."
For us these and their beneficial contents are as follows, in alphabetical order.

Fortunately, all but the globe artichokes and squash are easy to grow on small terraces. On a medium or large terrace individual globe artichoke plants could be grown in medium or large-sized pots or tubs and also as a row in a trough. Not only would you be able to

A BAKER'S DOZEN OF HEALTHY VEGETABLES

Vegetables	Beneficial Vitamin Mineral and Fibre Content
1 Artichokes	Vitamins C and minerals iron (Fe), phosphorus (P), potassium (K), calcium (C), folic acid and fibre
2 Beetroot	Mineral manganese (Mn) and anti-oxidant betacyanin
3 Broccoli	Vitamins A, C, K and folic acid
4 Carrots	Vitamin A and Beta carotene
5 Garlic	Vitamins C, B5, B6, Zn, K, C and minerals selenium (Se), iron (Fe), copper (Cu) and anti-oxidants.
6 Parsley	Vitamins A, C, K, iron (Fe) and folic acid
7 Peas	Vitamins A, C, B1, mineral potassium (K), folic acid and fibre
8 Onions	Vitamin A and anti-oxidants – sulphur etc.
9 Red lettuces	Vitamins C, K, folic acid, and anti-oxidants lutein and betacarotene
10 Swiss chard	Vitamins A, C, K and fibre
11 Shiitake mushrooms	Vitamins B,C, K and minerals manganese (Mn) and potassium (K) plus some protein
12 Squash	Vitamins B1, C, A and mineral (Mn)
13 Tomatoes	Vitamin C and anti-oxidant beta carotene

harvest some healthy artichokes to eat but the plants have interesting grey foliage and some artichoke buds – which could be left on the plants to produce large impressive blue flowers.

Plant breeders have bred miniature varieties of broccoli that take up about the same amount of room as a lettuce. Incidentally varieties of smaller than normal red lettuces and other vegetables are also now available. For starters look up such Internet mail order catalogues as Thompson and Morgan, Suttons Seeds, The Organic Catalogue and Kew Gardens — each have selections ideal for growing in containers.

Garlic cloves can be planted in pots on any terrace for harvesting the young shoots and entire young bulbs as they form for use in salads and omelettes and for flavouring cooked dishes. On a larger sunny terrace a bed of garlic to be nursed to produce mature fat garlic bulbs full of beneficial garlic oil could be grown in a large trough. In theory it could be raised on a growing table but this would be very much under-utilising the growing space from November until June.

Squash plants can be decorative as well as productive, but they take up rather a lot of space so traditional large varieties are out except for a fun plant on a large terrace. However, plant breeders have now produced miniature varieties that require less space and are suitable even for balconies as well as medium-sized terraces when grown along the ground or trained on the inside of railings. For productivity try growing red and oriental varieties of cut-and-come-again salad leaves or use red lettuce plantlets for harvesting individual leaves versus the total plant.

Although sprouting seeds are generally grown in a kitchen or spare bathroom, we add the growing of mix for the following reasons.

a. They all have high levels of vitamins and minerals. You will be eating some of the life creating vitamins and minerals which were built up and stored in the seeds when they were formed..

b. They take less than a week from seed packet to gourmet plate.

c. A stack of sprouting seed trays takes up less than the space of an A4 sheet of paper.

d. They can be grown in shady areas of terraces at temperatures of 15 to 25 degrees.

e. They can be covered with a domed mesh food cover to keep insects away.

We have grown the following seeds in tiered perforated sprouting trays, jars and fine mesh bags and very basic small kitchen trays as illustrated on pag XXX

1. Adzuki bean
2. Alfalfa
3. Beetroot
4. Broccoli
5. Cress
6. Chick peas
7. Fenugreek
8. Lentils
9. Mung bean
10. Mustard
11. Onion
12. Pumpkin
13. Radish
14. Rocket
15. Sunflower
16. Wheat

Instructions are normally given on the packets. Basic instructions are given in Part Two of *Growing Healthy Vegetables in Spain.*

9.4 What Can Be Added for Seasonal Diversity?

The world is then your oyster provided you have the space. The just mentioned book covers the growing of over a hundred types of vegetables (some of which have many suitable varieties) under Mediterranean climate conditions.

However for practical purposes we suggest the following list for your first expansions from the most healthy vegetables to additional ones that add seasonal diversity and the chance for even better home gastronomic eating.

This list includes some of the herbs included in Part Seven which we grow and use as salad vegetables as well as culinary and/or medicinal herbs.

Before buying seeds do check out the miniature (enano) varieties available locally and

1. Radishes	11. Climbing beans
2. New potatoes	12. Mini sweet corn
3. Spring onions	13. Peppers including Padrón peppers
4. Courgettes	14. Mini lettuces
5. Cucumbers	15. Cut and come again salad leaves
6. Aubergines	16. Mini cauliflowers
7. Mini butternut squash	17. Rocket
8. Broad beans	18. Parsley
9. Petit pois peas	19. Purslane
10. French beans	20. Nasturtiums

in mail order catalogues which include selections ideal for containers. These include Thompson and Morgan, Suttons and Kew Gardens - their Urban Collection.

9.5 How To Grow Vegetables in Containers

As indicated in Section 9.1, almost any container which is a minimum of 10 to 20cm deep can be used to grow vegetables. There are a few exceptions which have deeper roots such as artichokes, parsnips and sweet potatoes that require 50cm to do well. Naturally some containers are more aesthetic than others but their appearance can be disguised by surrounding them with flowering or evergreen plants.

If you regard any container you use as a mini raised bed or small area of a garden vegetable plot, everything falls into place. The success factors are common: selection of container, fertile compost, regular watering, watching out for pests and protecting green vegetables from the hottest suns. These are covered in turn in the sections that follow.

A.WHAT CONTAINERS ARE BEST USED?

We suggest the following for maximum convenience, provision of meaningful growing area, the provision of an ideal depth of soil for the roots of plants and minimising the rate at which moisture will be lost by evaporation.

a. Medium-sized pots, tubs, and other containers. Typically useful dimensions: Height 30 cm and width 30 cm.

b. Large-sized pots, tubs and other troughs. Typically useful dimensions: height 60 to 80cm, diameter or width 60 to 120cm and length of troughs 50 to 150cm.

c. Growing tables and raised beds. Typical dimensions: one to two metres long, 50 to 80cm wide and 20 to 25cm deep.

d. Grow bags

Typically, bags 80 x 30 x 10cm, holding 25 litres of compost, are now becoming more widely available in Spain. There are two types, one with a special compost mix for fruit vegetables such as tomatoes and peppers and another especially mixed for green vegetables such as lettuces. Both have marked holes for cutting open to plant plants. You could also use these composts in pots and other containers.

e. Planters

Wooden planters with fixed trellis work are useful for growing climbing beans peas cucumbers and tomatoes as shown on page 170.

All the above can be used for most vegetables. The exceptions being deep-rooted parsnips, potatoes, sweet potatoes, squash and globe artichokes which are best in 50cm-deep containers.

If you are growing vegetables on a covered terrace, rainwater will not fill and waterlog containers of compost. However, if you are growing vegetables on an open terrace heavy rain can soon waterlog lovingly cared-for plants.

Three things can be done.

- Ensure that all containers have good drainage holes. On a covered terrace no hole is a benefit as this ensures that the terrace floor remains dry after watering.

- Fix a mini plastic tent or tunnel supported by a wire or wood frame to keep heavy rain from entering on the pot. You can also use the cover for growing early crops or providing for frost and wind protection.

- Place a large tray under containers to collect water that drains through to be collected and used to water drier containers.

B. PRODUCTIVE COMPOST MIXES

It is very important that you have a good-quality compost for growing vegetables.
We suggest the following mixes for:

- Convenience of buying, transporting, mixing and storing bags /sacks of ingredients
- Reliability of products
- Ease of topping up the fertility of the compost between the harvest of one crop and the sowing/planting of the next.

Preferred mix

The mix we have had best success with when growing vegetables in containers is a mix of bagged worm compost or dried sheep goat or horse manure, a good potting compost preferable peat or soil-based and some gritty sand or grit in the proportions 1:8:1. The grit improves the drainage and aeration properties of the compost mix. Normal bag sizes are 20 or 50 litres for the worm compost, 20, 50 or 80 for the compost and 10 litres for the sand.

The amounts of compost mix required for typical containers are as follows.

- 30cm deep, 30cm diameter pot – 20 litres
- 50cm deep, 50cm diameter pot – 80 litres
- 40 x 50 x 10cm polystyrene fish box – 20 litres
- 20 x 60 x 20cm window box – 25 litres
- 30 x 40 x 30cm plastic storage box – 35 litres
- 100 x 80 x 20cm growing table – 150 litres
- 125 x 30 x 30cm trough – 200 litres.

If you have a mini worm composter, use the output of this. It also helps to add a half to one teaspoon of TerraCottem soil-improver to each litre of compost. This increases the water-holding capacity of the compost and at the same time can reduce watering needs by up to 50 per cent. Very useful in the summer months.

Other handy mixes and materials

You can buy grow bags and use the compost inside in pots and other containers. There are two types available, one especially mixed for growing fruit vegetables such as tomatoes and peppers and another for growing leaf vegetables such as lettuces.

Mini worm composters available include the well-known Bokashi ones (found at www. wigglywigglers.co.uk). They are only 37cm high and 30cm by 25cm wide. So your food and vegetable growing waste can be recycled as worm compost and a nutrient-rich fertiliser that is a by-product of the composter.

You can also use a sack of an unfertilized, peat-based compost and mix in 10 per cent of coarse sand. Then fertilize with an organic fertiliser.

B. PURCHASING PLANTLETS FOR CONVENIENCE AND PRODUCTIVITY

The easiest way to start growing vegetables on terraces and balconies is to buy plantlets, young plants grown ready for planting to save you the chore of growing from seed. Other benefits:

1. The time plants will be taking up valuable growing space from seed to harvest will be reduced by several weeks.

2. By buying plantlets such as lettuces and beetroots in batches you will be able to fill any gaps created when you harvest earlier plantings.

3. You will often be able to obtain greenhouse plantlets earlier than you can raise your own from seed, especially if living away from the coast.

When buying plantlets look out for grafted tomato pepper aubergine and melon plants. These are plants where the growth above the ground of one plant has been joined to the top of the roots of a stronger-growing variety to produce larger, stronger plants.

C. GROWING YOUR VEGETABLES FROM SEED

Many types of vegetables, including carrots and radishes, cannot be purchased as young plantlets as they do not transplant easily. Also the diversity of types and varieties will be restricted.

There are three ways of growing from seed.

a. Purchase prepared plastic trays or pots. You just remove the top, sow the seeds as instructed and water. In some cases the seeds are in impregnated paper which is already on the surface of the compost. When seedlings have two to four small leaves, they will need to be transplanted to larger containers. The first photograph shows an unopened pack for tomatoes, an open pack showing the bottom tray, the clear plastic mini greenhouse lid, a green bag of damp compost and a seed packet and a tray of tomato seedlings about to be transplanted to the individual pots. Instructions are given on the back of the label card.

b. Sow in 20cm diameter pots and thin out into larger containers when they have two to four leaves.

c. Sow directly into larger final containers. The disadvantage of this is that you will be taking up prime growing space for longer than 'b' in your larger pots, troughs and growing tables.

We suggest that you initially plant small seeds such as peppers and tomatoes in vermiculite and thin out into a compost prepared as described in Section B above. Vermiculite can be purchased in small bags in the better garden centres. Large seeds such as courgettes, cucumbers, beans and peas we would start off immediately in medium or large-sized containers in the compost mix of Section 8.6. Two seeds to a pot for courgettes and cucumbers for instance and some 10 or 12 peas and six to eight beans.

Ensure seeded pots are kept just damp. More water and the seedlings will rot. Two little and they will droop and dry out. If you have propolis (see Section 11.2), spray the compost with a dilute solution of this to prevent fungal attacks.

For more information see Section 5 that describes the growing of flowering plants from seed in more detail.

E. TIPS FOR GROWING IN MEDIUM-SIZE POTS, WINDOW BOXES AND TUBS

In general it makes best sense to dedicate each medium-sized container to a single variety of vegetables whether grown from seed or plantlets. Sow seeds thinly and plant small vegetable plantlets in groups but only one plant to a pot for large root ball, thirsty vegetable such as tomatoes. Many seedlings such as lettuces and carrots can be thinned for salads, allowing the rest to grow to maturity.

If you wish to be able to regroup or move empty containers to a storage area — perhaps under a growing table when not planted up — it is possible to fit pot supports with castors or use those that go under gas bottles.

F. TIPS FOR GROWING IN LARGER CONTAINERS

Maximise your harvests by mainly planting with purchased or homegrown plantlets. Grow your own plantlets in separate dedicated containers or a small propagator. Take account of the depth of the roots of various vegetables and locate shallow and deep-rooted vegetables adjacently so that one can feed on the nutrients in the top 5cm of compost and the adjacent vegetable in the deeper layers. For instance, shallow lettuces, deep carrots, shallow onions, deep

sweet potatoes, shallow radishes etc. can alternate in a pot. Ensure that your watering of the pots recognises this. Keep the deep roots as well as the shallow roots damp at all times. In the three large pots in the photograph the vegetables growing were as follows:

Pot 1: Tomato, salad leaves, lettuces, radishes and carrots.

Pot 2: Nasturtiums for salads, onions, garlic, and sweet potatoes with tubers half way down the pot with the leaves growing down the side of the pot through the railings. When everything else had been eaten, we dug down into the compost and harvested a dozen reasonable-sized potatoes.

Pot 3: Tomatoes, peppers, climbing beans and a courgette plant trailing down the side.

Not the greatest harvest of all varieties of vegetables grown, but it proved what can be done in a small space and three pots picked up at the dustbins. This saved money but they are available from horticultural supplies or the better stocked garden centres. If not, offer to purchase some second-hand ones they have used to deliver palms or order new ones.

If you prepare your compost well before planting, you will only need to give fruit vegetable crops such as tomatoes and peppers supplementary feeds. Plus a half-year top-up between plantings with an inch of worm compost mixed into the top 20cm between plantings.

G. TIPS FOR GROWING ON GROWING TABLES

Growing tables can provide a single sizeable growing area of half to two square metres. Keep them fully sown and planted at all times. Grow smallish plants closely on tables and plant larger vegetable plants in separate containers for maximum productivity.

Growing tables were originally developed for use on covered terraces as if in the open and, if it rains heavily, the compost can flood and waterlog the roots of plants. We therefore recommend that, when us tables on an open terrace, you cut a 2cm hole in the centre of the base to allow excess rain water to drain into a small dustbin below. This water can the be used later for watering when the compost has dried out.

When filled with compost, construct a mini poly tunnel by weighting plastic sheeting over a series of string wire hoops. This will stop the table becoming flooded and bring on crops faster.

Top up the fertility level after each crop with supplementary additions of worm compost or a general slow release ecological fertiliser.

A trellis panel can be fitted to one or two sides to support tomatoes cucumbers and dwarf climbing beans in the summer and climbing peas during the winter.

H. SOWING AND PLANTING DISTANCES

As you will have limited space and in many cases will be harvesting young vegetables rather than let them get to full size, you can plant much closer than you would do in a vegetable plot for maximum productivity.

For instance:

- Sow carrot seeds closely in a block . As soon as young carrots are 2cm long, thin out the plants and use the mini carrots for salads. The ones left will grow quicker and to a larger size.

- Sow cut-and-come-again salad leaves thinly. If too close, eat a few young plants. If too sparse, sow more densely next time.

- Plant small lettuces 15cm apart and eat when they start to touch each other. Initially eat the alternate ones and let the others grow for a while.

- You can also harvest the outside leaves as if they are cut and come again salad leaves.

- Plant tomatoes peppers and aubergines in individual pots or plant 15cm apart if mini varieties or 20cm apart if regular varieties in troughs.

- Sow three seeds of cucumbers, mini squash and courgettes in individual pots or at the edge of a large 70 to 100cm-diameter pots so that the growing foliage can be trained down the side of the pots leaving the centre clear for other types of vegetables.

- A few peas can be sown in a window box of flowering plants over winter. Not much of a harvest but the chance for one meal of freshly picked peas before they lose their wonderful fresh natural perfumes and taste. And the flowers and ripening peas look attractive on the windowsill.

I. GROWING MUSHROOMS

Many claims are made for the nutritional and medicinal properties of various types of cultivated and edible wild mushrooms (setas in Spanish). However, many people do not know which of the wild woodland varieties are edible so it can be dangerous to go on autumn wild mushroom-hunting trips. And in any case good mushroom grounds are kept a secret or controlled in some Mediterranean areas.

Luckily there is an easy solution which is becoming increasingly popular. Some varieties can be grown on a small scale on a shady apartment terrace as well as in a kitchen, bathroom or garage using specially prepared plastic-covered spawn-impregnated blocks.

Each is about 35cm by 45cm so takes up little space. The blocks can be purchased in many agricultural cooperatives, animal feed warehouses or garden centres.

We have seen the following varieties of mushrooms for sale in Spain and know that a similar range is available in other Mediterranean countries.

- Cultivated mushrooms (champiñones) that are best grown in a dark cellar, under build or garage.
- Wild mushrooms (setas) in the following varieties – shitake de salud, niscalo, boleto, chopo, cardo, oyster and miele.

The optimum temperatures are between 10 and 25 degrees but they will grow at down to 3 degrees. From our experience there is an advantage in growing at a lower temperature as the crops mature more slowly and one doesn't get a massive crop all at once. A single block can produce up to 15 to 20 kilos over a period of several months and all you need to do is to tear a few holes in the top of the bag and water or not water according to the instructions for each type of mushroom. It will be beneficial to place some impregnated blocks inside a large cardboard box to reduce the light. If too many mushrooms mature at one time, they can be made into soup, frozen or dried. The only problem you might meet is that your bag has been in stock for some weeks before you purchased it and has already yielded a crop or two. It is worth ordering in advance so that you get the variety you want and are informed as soon as they are in stock.

9.6 Dealing With Problems

If you grow vegetables in the isolation of an apartment terrace and don't force your plants by over-watering, you should have few problems with insect and fungal problems. However, in case you do suddenly see insects around or leaves going brown due to a fungal attack, we give photographs to help you identify the problem and suggest treatments in Section 10.2.

If you see plants suddenly flopping over, you have probably forgotten to water them for a few days or have not increased your watering as the temperature rises from spring to summer. This is especially important if you have recently sown seeds or planted young plantlets. In mid-summer the temperature of direct sunlight on plants is very much higher than the shade temperatures reported and forecast in weather forecasts, the same when you are sunbathing. Tomatoes, peppers and aubergines for instance will love this, but some especially leaf vegetables such as lettuces, spinach and Swiss chard will not and will wither or go fast to seed. So, if you decide to grow these during the summer months, do so on a north-east or west-facing terrace and, if possible, shade your vegetable-growing terrace with a blind during the hottest hours of direct reflected light. Within a year you will have discovered the variations in the microclimate of your specific terrace or terraces as it affects growing vegetables.

Wash the outsides of containers with dilute vinegar and water a couple of times a year to avoid fungal problems.

Cats and dogs are not a major problem in most vegetable gardens, but your large containers and growing tables might just be an attraction if you have a cat or dog and — as we discovered in one Barcelona apartment — a pet cockerel. So separate the vegetable and pet areas or provide some form of protection.

9.7 Storing Your Harvests

Two of the main objectives for growing vegetables on your terrace are that you can harvest them just before preparing a salad, a salad sandwich or cooking them and that you grow them in a way that avoids gluts. However, there will be occasions when you need to harvest in the morning for the day and too many of your plants mature at the same time. So what can you do to get the best out of your short-term excesses and not loose their valuable vitamin and mineral contents?

1. Leaf Vegetables - Place green leaved vegetables in the salad compartment of your fridge. Many modern fridges now have a climate-controlled section. Half-used lettuces are best wrapped in damp kitchen towel paper or a cloth.

2. Flower Vegetables – Hopefully you will have grown some mini broccoli or cauliflowers. Do the same as for leaf vegetables.

3. Root Vegetables If you have grown some new potatoes in a container or specially designed tower, only harvest what you need that day. They will keep better in the compost they were grown in. Likewise with carrots and radishes. Start to harvest them when just large enough to eat raw in salads and progressively harvest larger ones each week as they grow for salads and cooking. In this way you are unlikely to have a glut of large carrots that need harvesting and storing. At the end the last carrots can be kept firm and fresh by placing the roots up to the height of the stem in a container in which they can stand upright such as a mug or two. Sprouting seeds can be stored for up to five days in the chill drawer of a refrigerator. If your production will not be used in this time freeze your estimated excess as soon as you harvest a batch of sprouting seeds.

4. Fruit Vegetables – Tomato and pepper plantss are the most prolific producers so are the most likely to produce gluts. Peppers and aubergines can normally be left for a few more days on the bushes, but tomatoes can become over-ripe.

Tomatoes can be frozen for winter use and tomato jam is a favourite Mediterranean conserve. You can also dry tomatoes under the hot sun or dry them in a slightly warm oven or proprietary tray drier, which can be used 365 days a year to dry also surplus herbs mushrooms and health biscuits.

5. Mushrooms – The timing and size of mushroom crops are difficult to control and once an impregnated bag or box starts to sprout oyster and shitake mushrooms, for instance, the production will become more than two people can eat totally fresh — unless one lives on nothing else than fried mushrooms, mushroom soup, mushroom omelettes and mushroom-flavoured casseroles. We freeze and dry excesses.

9.8 Mini Vegetable-Growing is Great For Children

There is a worldwide concern that children even more than adults eat too few vegetables and many surveys in schools indicate that an amazing number of children cannot identify a common selection of vegetables or explain where they come from apart from a jar, tin or freezer bag.

So, if you have children living in your apartment, do encourage them to become involved in the small-scale growing of vegetables. Either helping you or doing it themselves with supervision. If you have a small terrace as well as a main large terrace, you could dedicate the smaller one to their vegetable-growing activities. The benefits will be educational, better eating habits, fun and as with us it can develop into a lifetime interest in growing things and self-sufficiency. Hopefully, within a short time they will tell their friends that growing their own crops is cool and a Growing Circle as discussed in Section 1.10 might emerge among their friends, or a more worthwhile school gardening club.

Children of all ages can be fascinated by watching things grow and learning how to use them. Indeed, a growing table would be a wonderful way to start children off. But, if you cannot afford one or lack the space, try a trough, window box, pots or just a tray for sprouting seeds.

To achieve commitment it's important that children start to grow things that they can relate to and be willing to eat and then expand the range of crops with experimental eating.

How about the following for starter activities?
a. Grow batches of sprouting seeds in a plastic container or tray and add them to a salad, sandwich or help mother cook those spring rolls that they enjoy at the Chinese restaurant.

b. Buy some lettuce plantlets to plant in a growing table, window box or trough. Let them harvest leaves as the plants grow to experience the difference between young and mature leaves. They could follow this up with the growing of cut and come again salad leaves.

c. Plant and care for a cherry tomato plant in a plastic container. Cherry tomatoes are small, colourful and, when ripe, tasty and full of juice. Just the fruit for children to cut their teeth on.

d. Start to grow easily germinated vegetables such as radishes and carrots in a pot or preferably as their first seed-grown vegetables on the growing table. They will learn that some seeds take longer than others to germinate and therefore need more patience.

e. Sow and grow peas in an old toy box or other large plastic container. When the pods fill out they will love harvesting and podding them when just ripe to eat. Half may not reach the saucepan!

f. Care for a pot of mint. They can pick the leaves for a *poleo menta* infusion and mother's new potatoes or mint sauce.

g. Sow and care for a giant sunflower plant. Let them see how tall they can grow and how large the flower can develop. If they are lucky, the seeds will fatten out ready to be dried and shelled as a snack. Alternatively the seeds can be used as food for wild birds.

h. If they like garlic, let them separate the garlic cloves corms from a complete head of garlic and then plant them just so that the tops show in a large container. This is best done in November. The green garlic stems that grow can be used in salads or the plants can be nursed to maturity in mid summer.

i. A more challenging project would be to grow peanuts in a 50cm-wide, 30cm-deep plastic container. All they need to do is to plant six to eight seeds in May from a dried but unsalted pod. An interesting plant will grow up and when it dies back in the early autumn the compost can be tipped out on to a sheet of newspaper and the peanuts harvested from the roots to which they will be attached. Once washed and dried, a recognisable home grown snack is ready.

To get the most from such activities ensure that children are provided with a good compost mix which they always keep damp and a plastic bottle of already-diluted, ecological, vegetable fertiliser to feed the plants with a fine-spouted watering can.

If a group of friends show interest, competitions could be held for the best vegetables and tallest sunflower grown.

Dealing with plant and tree pests and diseases

Practical ways of dealing with the problems and diseases you may meet when growing trees and plants, from flowering and evergreen to fruit, herbs and vegetables.

10.1 Typical Problems and Diseases

A. LIKELIHOOD OF PEST AND FUNGAL DISEASES

As mentioned in Section 1.1 gardening on terraces, balconies and windowsills is in many ways easier than developing and maintaining a garden around a villa. There are four reasons for this in relation to serious insect and fungal attacks.

- You are probably not exposed to the outbreaks of pests and diseases that often develop on abandoned vegetable and fruit-growing land.

- With less than 20 per cent of planted terraces, balconies and window boxes, infestations from neighbours are less likely than in a densely planted urbanisation.

- The higher your apartment the less likely it is that fungal spores will be in the air and the lower the passing population of harmful insects.

- With only a relatively small number of plants to care for it should be possible to follow the advice given in earlier sections of the book to avoid under or over-watering and over-feeding your plants These three things alone will minimise the occurrences of pest attacks and fungal diseases on flowering and evergreen plants, fruit trees, herbs or vegetables.

However, from time to time your plants and trees will experience insect and fungal attacks. Some may come in with the plants you buy and appear fairly quickly while others may appear at any time. Even a plant 10 years of age may suddenly fail for no immediate apparent reason.

We will now look at some general preventive measures you can take followed by what to do about the 12 problems you are most likely to meet.

B. SOME GENERAL PREVENTATIVE MEASURES

On a preventive basis we would:

▲ Insect catchers   ▲ Spraying plants

- Stick proprietary, sticky, yellow flying-insect-catchers (*trampas*) in plant pots and among growing vegetables and on fruit trees. This will reduce the number of insects that need to be combated by spraying.

- Plant some garlic cloves in plant pots. The smell will not be noticeable to you but many insects will go elsewhere.

• Mix neem powder into the surface of compost in pots. Will be found on www.trabe.net.

• Spray plants monthly with neem oil in water. Weekly on geraniums throughout the year.

• Wrap traditional grease bands around the trunks of fruit trees in the autumn.

• Dust fruit vegetables such tomatoes and courgettes fortnightly with yellow sulphur powder shaken through an old sock. Also vine fruits.

• Most importantly avoid over-watering or over-feeding plants to avoid the weak fast growth that often attracts insects and fungal spores.

• Avoid co-planting thirsty and drought-resistant plants in the same container as one could be over-watered and one under-watered.

• Avoid locating tropical plants that require regular misting near to plants susceptible to fungal attacks as a result of high humidity.

C. THE MOST COMMON INSECT AND FUNGAL ATTACKS

The thirteen most likely problems you will meet are as follows.

Insect Attacks	
1. Aphids	8. Scale
2. Citrus leaf miner	9. Slugs and snails
3. Geranium moth	
4. Leaf curl	**Fungal Attacks**
5. Mediterranean fruit flies and moths	1. Honey fungus
6. Mealy bug	2. Mildew
7. Red spider mite	3. Rotting off
	4. Sooty leaves

Effective ecological ways of combating these are discussed in the next two sections. We recommend these rather than more hazardous chemical solutions to minimise the risk of polluting the small area of an apartment.

We give our preferred ecological solutions as they are:

a. now widely available.

b. safer for the family pets and neighbours especially in small terrace and balcony spaces.

c. Now supported by the EU which each year bans more and more of the previous generations of inorganic chemical products.

Some of the brand names to look out for are Compo, Floraguard, Neudorff, Seipasa and Trabe.

Also remember that prior to the availability of industrial products many grandparents used cooled infusions of garlic, lavender, melissa, mint, nasturtium, rue, scented geranium and thyme leaves as general insecticides; sage and horsetail as fungicides; and dandelion, nettle, comfrey and borage as soil and foliar fertilisers. Most of the leaves can normally be obtained from herb stalls in markets and good health stores.

Our guidelines for preparing the home-made solutions mentioned in the charts that follow are as follows:

- Herbal infusions – prepare as you would a cup of tea and cool before use.
- Neem oil – Add 5cc to a litre of water.
- Propolis – Add 5cc to a litre of water.
- Potassium soap – Dissolve 100gr in five litres of hot water.
- Washing up liquid – Mix five drops into a litre of water.

The tables are designed so that you can start to search for solutions by either going to the name of the problem if you already know it or start by looking through the descriptions to find one that describes the problem you have. The problems in each section are in alphabetical order.

D. COMBATING INSECT ATTACKS

▲ Aphids   ▲ Citrus tree miner   ▲ Leaf curl

▲ Mealy bugs   ▲ Fruit fly traps   ▲ Scale

The Most Common Insect Problems

What does it look like?	What plants can be affected?	What can cause it?	What can you do about it?
APHIDS Pulgones **a. Greenfly, Mosca verde.** Countless tiny sticky green flies on stems, leaves and flower buds. Often ants seen on their sweet sticky excretion.	Oleanders, roses, lady of the night, chrysanthemums, hibiscus, citrus trees, also apple, pear and apricots, plus beans and artichokes.	All three can appear when plants are allowed to dry out and excess nitrogen feeds are given which result in weak new growth. Some plants are also natural foods for the insects.	a. Spray twice-weekly with solutions of potassium soap/eco washing-up water or neem oil in water. b. Clean off with old tooth brush dipped in washing up liquid or potassium soap solution. c. Place yellow sticky traps near infestations.
b. Whitefly, Mosca blanca. Tiny white insects covering under sides of leaves with a sticky film and black mould. Touch a leaf and you might set off a cloud of tiny white flies.	Geraniums, begonias, and what were called indoor plants in the UK plus broccoli and other brassicas vegetables.		As above plus: Place plastic bottles lined with bright yellow paint near plants – yellow deters the flies.
c. Blackfly, Mosca negra. Groups of tiny black insects on new tips and stems.	Nasturtiums, broad beans, spinach, artichokes and swiss chard.		As above plus: Place a basil or mint plant near by as a natural deterrent.
CITRUS LEAF MINER Minador de cítricos Curling of leaves, small holes in leaves and signs of burrowing on underside of leaves.	All types of citrus fruit trees.	Natural attraction to citrus trees. Probably not totally curable.	a. Cut off affected leaves. b. Spray in spring and autumn with a mix of neem and a natural foliar feed. We use a cooled infusion made with dried nettle leaves.
GERANIUM MOTH Mosca Africana Small black holes in stems where eggs have been laid and small brown moth hovering around plants.	Zonal and ivy leaved geraniums but not the graveolens varieties.	Over-feeding and watering producing weak soft fleshy growth. Infestation from nearby plants.	a.Place a graveolens geranium plant amongst other varieties or spray with geranium oil in water. b. Plant garlic cloves in pots as an inhibitor or spray with a garlic water solution. (continued over)

The Most Common Insect Problems

What does it look like?	What plants can be affected?	What can cause it?	What can you do about it?
			c. Spray with a proprietary product. d. Spray twice weekly March to November with a neem oil in water solution.
LEAF CURL Abolladora, lepra Blistering and curling up of leaves which shrivel and fall off.	Mostly affected are peaches, plums and nectarines.	Fungal spores washed by rain from bark of trees.	a. Remove affected and fallen leaves. b. Give affected trees a nitrogen foliar feed. c. Spray with a neem oil/propolis/nettle mix fortnightly from autumn to early spring.
MEDITERRANEAN FRUIT FLIES AND MOTHS Mosca de la fruita, lepidopteros, zeurzero, hoplocampa, mancha negra and el greening.	Mostly stone and pip fruits including citrus fruits, apples, pears, plums and olives.	Attracted by aromas to feed and breed.	a. Spray fortnightly all year with neem oil and potassium soap mixes or general eco insecticide. b. Fit grease bands to tree trunks in autumn/winter. c. Remove fallen fruit from top of compost and floor. d. Don't overfeed/water. e. Hang fly traps.
MEALY BUG/ WOOLY APHIDS Cochinilla Sticky white bugs on stems and underside of leaves.	Stephanotis, euonymus, succulents, indoor type plants and bougainvilleas, citrus and apple trees etc.	Dense foliage with no light, weak plants and over-watering.	a. Don't co-plant thirsty and drought-resistant plants. b.Clean off with paint brush or kitchen towel soaked in soapy water. c. Spray weekly with soapy water solution or neem oil in water.

The Most Common Insect Problems

What does it look like?	What plants can be affected?	What can cause it?	What can you do about it?
RED SPIDER MITE Acaro Yellow speckled leaves and leaf fall. Also underside of leaves coated with a silk-like web and tiny spiders.	Generally citrus, apples, roses, ficus, oleander, annuals and semi-tropical plants regarded as indoor plants in the UK.	High temperatures and over-feeding with fertilisers rich in nitrogen.	a. Where possible wipe off with kitchen towel or paint brush soaked in a neem/propolis/soap mix. b. Spray with a neem oil or potassium soap or eco washing-up liquid and water mix.
SCALE Escama Hard scales on leaves and stems.	Bay, oleander, succulents, Christmas cacti, oleander and citrus trees.	Lack of light and humid conditions.	a. Wipe with propolis or horsetail solutions. b. Spay weekly with a neem oil and propolis or potassium soap solution.
SLUGS AND SNAILS Babosas and caracoles Slugs – remains of eaten plants and live slugs and their slimy trails. Snails – Bitten leaves and stems, slimy trails, live snails moving around and stuck to outside of containers in the shade.	Young annuals, vegetables, fleshy plants and some succulents. Seedlings very vulnerable.	Can come in with new plants, sometimes on bags of compost and on the outside or inside of new containers. Also on leaf vegetables from markets.	a. Check plants, sacks of compost and containers before you buy them. b. Place saucers of beer amongst plant pots and on the surface of the compost in larger containers. c. Sprinkle an ecological slug/snail bait on surface of compost and between containers. d. Collect and squash any you see.

E. COMBATING FUNGAL ATTACKS

▲ Honey fungus   ▲ Mildew   ▲ Rotting off   ▲ Sooty Leaves

1. HONEY FUNGUS
Hongo del miel.

What does it look like: Sticky golden drips/lumps of a sticky jelly-like substance oozing out of branches and trunks.

What plants are affected: Stone and fruit trees.

What can cause it: Wind and bird-borne fungal spores.

What can you do about it:
    a. Prune off badly affected and dead branches.

    b. Spray with fungicide/foliar feed mix like a neem oil/propolis/nettle cocktail in water.

    c. If really bad, scrub off with a toothbrush soaked in the above solution. Repeat fortnightly until the problem is cured.

2. MILDEW
Mildiu/oidio. There are varieties called downy and powdery.

What does it look like: Pale yellow blotches and/or white powder on leaves.

What plants are affected: Annuals, geraniums, chrysanthemums, apples, vines, tomatoes, onions, garlic, cucumbers and courgettes.

What can cause it: A combination of damp conditions and high temperatures.

What can you do about it:
    a. Avoid watering leaves.

    b. Dust plants fortnightly – especially the leaves - with yellow sulphur powder (*azufre*) shaken through an old sock.

    c. A neem/propolis or horsetail spray can also help.

3. ROTTING OFF
Depudricion

What does it look like: Discoloured wilting leaves, browny-grey mushy strawberries.

What plants are affected: Roses, oleanders, annuals, succulents, hedging plants, indoor plant types and strawberries.

What causes it: The waterlogging of containers. On uncovered terraces due to heavy rainfall and on uncovered and covered ones due to regular over-watering.

What can you do about it:

Preventive actions:

a. Ensure that the drainage holes in the base of containers are unblocked when purchased. If not, cut or drill them out. If the holes seem small for the size of pot, enlarge them.

b. Place stones or pieces of broken pots/crockery in a 2 cm heap over the drainage holes before filling up with compost.

c. Ensure you use a water-retaining but well-draining compost. Include sand or grit in the compost mix before filling containers.

d. Drill small holes in the lower side of window boxes just above the base or the top of the inbuilt water reservoir. If done before you fill the window boxes place a small pile of stones on the inside of the hole before filling with compost. Push a cork into the hole on the outside. This can be used to drain off excess water.

e. Lay pots and tubs on their side to drain off excess water if they become waterlogged.

f. When growing flowers and vegetables from seed, spray the surface of the compost and seedlings with a propolis or cooled horsetail infusion to prevent the stems from rotting where they emerge from the compost.

g. Remove any dead plants to avoid a spread of the problem to nearby plants.

h. Don't use the compost in affected pots without first sterilising it on a tray in an oven or throw it away.

Corrective actions

a. Stop watering and don't restart until the compost is almost dried out.

b. Spray affected areas with a strong propolis solution and spray the foliage with a nitrogen foliar feed such as a cooled nettle leaf infusion.

4. SOOTY LEAVES

La negrilla

What does it look like: Leaves covered with a fine black sooty deposit that prevents leaves from breathing and reduces photosynthesis.

What plants are affected: Bay, oleander, stephanotis, succulents, Christmas cacti, and citrus trees.

What causes it: Lack of light and humidity. Often associated with scale and mealy bugs.

What can you do about it:

a. If a small tree is affected clean the leaves with a toothbrush and potassium soap or neem oil solutions in water. Can take several treatments to eradicate.

b. Larger trees can be sprayed with a strong jet of the same solutions.

10.5 Leaf Burn

If your apartment is in an exposed position and liable to have cold winter winds from snowy mountain areas or sleet or hail, the ends of leaves and in worst cases whole leaves and small branches can be burnt. That means that leaves will go brown and dry and the ends of branches can die back. The best thing is to leave the damage until the spring and then prune off the damaged parts of the plant and trim surviving or new growth back to a good shape. Then give a nitrogen-rich foliar feed to encourage strong new growth. In addition, scorching hot summer winds can burn some of the more delicate evergreen plants.

10.3 Quick Hints and Tips for Healthy Plants

This is a compilation of some of the essential advice included in the book.

1. Many plants die from 'overwatering' because surface compost has no chance to dry out between watering so the pots become waterlogged and also by 'underwatering' because compost is allowed to dry out completely making it impossible to re-absorb enough moisture to save plant .

2. Water gently – allowing water to soak in. Wait a few minutes and then water again.

3. Improve water for acid-loving plants such as azaleas and hydrangeas by adding a few drops of vinegar to a litre of water

4. Plants such as cyclamen and Christmas cacti like to be watered from a drip tray placed under the pot which has a layer of grit or small pebbles which one covers with water.

5. Plants listed in Section 4.2 as needing little water will survive best if planted in a sandy, free-draining compost rather than pure peat .

6. Annuals will always need to be kept moist. Perennials need moderate watering – surface can dry out between watering. A lot depends on the quality of the potting compost/soil.

7. Once temperatures drop in winter reduce your watering on all plants. Especially if there is a chance of frost.

8. Erratic watering can cause leaf drop.

9. Brown patches on leaves can be caused by under-watering and drying winds. Increase watering and mist-spray leaves during hot and windy periods.

10. Dust and clean shiny-leafed plants. Remove dust with small paint brush and wipe with equal mix of beer and milk.

11. Cacti – plant in light, free-draining soil, place in full sun, mist in hot weather. If over-watered will rot and be prone to infestations and fungal diseases.

12. Succulents – plant in light, free-draining soil, do well in full sun and semi shade.

13. Sub-tropical house plants – keep moist and mist in hot weather. Avoid direct sunlight.

14. Don't co-plant thirsty plants with drought-resistant plants.

15. If variegated plants don't have enough light leaf colour will revert to green.

16. Deadheading means using scissors or small secateurs to cut off dead flowers being careful not to cut out new buds.

17. Feed non-flowering plants with nitrogen-high feed and flowering plants with feed high in potassium/potash, especially in the growing season from spring to autumn.

18. Over-feeding and over-watering produce weak sappy plants which are prone to diseases and insect infestations, especially mealy bug.

19. Night water (urine) diluted with 10 times as much water is a good source of nitrogen. Least expensive fertiliser available.

20. Most effective ecological insecticides are neem oil, dried nettle and thyme infusions and soapy water.

21. For fungal and viral infections spray with horsetail, seaweed and propolis mix which will cure problems and strengthen plants.

22. Plant insect deterrents amongst your pots such as lemon verbena, French marigolds, geranium graveolens, marigolds, nasturtiums and thyme. Use bay leaves to keep cockroaches away and orange peel to keep cats off your pots.

23. When growing vegetables feed the soil rather than the plants.

24. Remember stay green. We don't like being showered with bad chemicals so why should your plants be any different? The natural insecticides and fungicides mentioned previously can be found in natural products, i.e. neem in toothpaste and shampoo, just as nettle can combat hair loss and gout and propolis treat colds and gum infections and cold sores.

25. Talk to your plants.

Seasonal calendars

These season-by-season calendars will remind you of the important tasks that need to be carried out in apartment gardens. Calendars are organised by seasons as there can be up to a month's difference between the beginning and end of spring, autumn and winter, depending on where you are located – southern or northern Costas, beach or high inland valleys, south-facing or north-facing sides of mountain ridges.

11.1 Spring

Cool and warm conditions. The time to stimulate plants into growth and plant new ones and prepare for the coming hot summer conditions. And the time to enjoy seasonal harvests.

FLOWERING PLANTS

1. Buy and plant spring/summer annuals and new perennial plants.
2. Start to increase watering as the weather warms up.
3. Re-pot root bound plants.
4. Sprinkle ecological snail and slug bait on the drainage trays of vulnerable plants if you see a slimy snail trail or nibbled leaves. They can come in with new plants from a garden centre, buried in the compost.
5. Give plants a spring feed. Adding a fertiliser pearl or stick is an easy way of doing this.
6. Watch out for signs of insect infestations as the temperature rises and treat as per Part Ten. Spray geranium plants every week until the late autumn. Place a yellow sticky insect trap in a number of plant pots to catch the several flying insects attracted to yellow – especially aphids.
7. Move plants over-wintered in sheltered spots back to normal locations.

EVERGREEN PLANTS

1. Clean the leaves with a 1:1 beer and milk mix.
2. Increase watering gradually as temperatures rise.
3. Clean off dead leaves from surface of compost and loosen top three centimetres.
3. Spray surface of soil and bottom of trunks against fungal attacks.
4. Trim plants to desired size and shape.
5. Spray with a nettle infusion to strengthen plants.

HERBS

1. Clean containers of winter grime.
2. Trim untidy growth and any dead bits.
3. Clean surface of compost and loosen top 3cm of compost.
4. Buy a selection of new herbs.
5. Buy herb starter kits or packets of seeds for annuals and start them off.
6. Plant out seedlings into larger containers.
7. Replace any unhealthy plants in herb barrel.

FRUIT GROWING

1. Buy and plant new citrus and other sub-tropical fruit trees..
2. Prune existing citrus trees once they are in flower .
3. Start to increase watering to all fruit trees and plants.
4. Start to spray trees and plants monthly with a neem oil, propolis and water mix.
5. Plant a strawberry barrel.
6. Dust strawberries with sulphur powder against mildew.

VEGETABLE GROWING

1. Clear out end of over-wintered crops.
2. Plant plantlets and sow seeds for spring and summer crops.
3. Set up mini watering system for regular use or when away.
4. Dust fruit-type vegetable plants with sulphur powder against mildew.
5. Shake some ecological snail and slug bait around vegetable-growing containers.
6. Place cut-off 5 or 7-litre water bottles over recently sown seeds and just-planted young fruit and vegetable plants until weather warms up.
7. Collect containers to expand on last year's production.

OTHER

1. Have blinds and/or awning fitted ready for hotter suns.
2. Repaint terrace walls and railings.
3. Spring-clean tiled floors and walls.
4. Clean terrace furniture.
5. Start to eat out more on the terrace.

11.2 Summer

Hot and very hot. The time for attentive care and attention to plants – especially on south-facing terraces, balconies and windowsills – to help the plants survive until the cooler Autumn. And the time to enjoy summer harvests.

FLOWERING PLANTS

1. Double or even treble watering as the hottest days arrive.
2. Deadhead annuals and perennials to stimulate continuous flowering.
3. Mist-spray plants late evening.
4. Use blinds and awnings to protect plants during hottest hours.

5. Check that watering system is not leaking and is working correctly.

6. Watch out for pest and fungi problems and treat as per part ten.

7. Fix wires or trellis for new climbing plants.

EVERGREEN PLANTS

1. Watch out for mealy bugs and scale and treat as Section 10.2 if they appear.

2. Watch that drooping and falling leaves don't signify under watering.

3. Watch that yellowing of leaves and a white ring around the bottom of the trunk don't signify over watering.

4. Mist spray leaves fortnightly.

5. If leaves become dirty clean with a one to one beer and milk mix.

HERBS

1. Ensure compost does not dry out.

2. Watch out for insects and deal with any immediately.

3. Harvest herbs regularly to stimulate new young growth.

4. If you can't keep up with plants growth harvest for hanging up in bunches

or freezing in ice trays..

5. Move herbs that have been in full sun into semi-shade.

6. Pot on maturing young plants.

FRUIT GROWING

1. If heavily laden thin out fruit to increase size of fruit.

2. Thin out excessive growth of vines and non fruiting branches.

3. Keep up monthly neem/propolis spraying of trees and sulphur dusting of vines.

4. Double or even triple watering as weather becomes hotter and hotter.

5. Prune deciduous fruit trees to stimulate flowering buds for next year.

6. Place ecological slug bait around strawberry barrel.

7. Dry excess summer crops for winter use.

VEGETABLE GROWING

1. Ensure composts are damp at all times.

2. Dust fruit vegetable plants – tomatoes cucumbers etc. – with sulphur powder every two weeks.

3. Give fruit vegetables a fortnightly potassium rich summer feed.

4. Give green vegetables an ecological high in nitrogen feed to the surface of the compost or by mist spraying the leaves.

5. Shade lettuces and other leaf vegetables from the hottest suns.

6. Spray green vegetables with a neem/nettle mix.

7. Sow seeds for winter broccoli, cauliflowers and other mini brassicas to produce plantlets for planting out in October in largish containers including rows on a growing table.

OTHER

1. Set up mini water feature.

2. Build gazebo on open terraces for shade.

3. Set up a growing table for starting a collection of succulents or cacti.

4. Fix a water butt and guttering in readiness for autumn rains.

5. Build chicken or quail house.

11.3 Autumn

Hot to cool. The time for keeping plants flowering and enjoy seasonal harvests.

FLOWERING PLANTS

1. Cut back watering as weather cools.

2. Change summer annuals for autumn/winter annuals.

3. Plant winter and spring bulbs.

4. Place new fertiliser pearls in those plants that continue to grow and flower and don't go dormant.

5. In frost vulnerable areas place fleece over tender plants.

6. Take cuttings and propagate new plants.

7. Sprinkle ecological snail and slug bait on drip trays under pots.

EVERGREEN PLANTS

1. Clean from summer dust with a beer/milk 1:1 solution..

2. Clean fallen leaves from top of compost.

3. Loosen surface soil in containers.

4. Cut back watering as weather cools.

5. Take cuttings to propagate new plants.

6. Trim to shape if untidy growth.

7. Replant root bound plants in larger containers.

HERBS

1. Take cuttings to produce new plants by the spring.
2. Remove flower buds on annuals to prolong growth and harvesting.
3. Ensure containers do not become waterlogged during autumn rains.
4. Harvest final leaf crops from annual herbs.
5. Keep seeds for culinary use and sowing next spring.
6. Trim perennials so that they do not become leggy and straggly over the winter.
7. Move the most delicate herbs into sheltered positions for the winter months.

FRUIT

1. Keep up the monthly sprayings against insects and fungal spores.
2. Buy tubs and plant up additional fruit trees.
3. Fix grease bands to the trunks of trees.
4. Harvest autumn fruits as they become ripe.
5. Clean up fallen leaves and fruit from top of compost and floor tiles.
6. Loosen top layer of compost in containers.
7. Check/change canes and supports for fruit trees and vines.

VEGETABLES

1. Clear out finished summer crops and prepare containers for next crops.
2. Start off autumn/over wintering seeds and plantlets.
3. Continue to dust tomatoes, peppers and aubergines with sulphur.
4. Fill additional containers with compost to expand production.
5. Plant a potato barrel in early October for Christmas potatoes.
6. Start to grow sprouting seeds and micro vegetables with cooler weather.
7. Buy spore-impregnated grow bag for wild mushrooms.

OTHER

1. Start project for fitting planters and trellis around the open terrace.
2. Widen narrow windowsills with shelving planks to hold larger containers.
3. Install a storage shed or cupboard for gardening things and terrace furniture.
4. Check under terrace chairs and tables for small wasp nests.
5. Clean and seal terrace tiles.

11.4 Winter

Cool to cold with periods of hot spring-like days.

FLOWERING PLANTS

1. Protect plants from low winter sun with blind or awning.
2. Reduce watering to minimum to keep plants healthy.
3. Clean containers if grimy and remove any dead material from tops of compost..
4. Check that ties are not tight on trunks and branches.
5. Buy seasonal plants for year-end festive displays and give special care.
6. Winter cut-back of vines, shrubs and trees to keep to sensible size.
7. Take succulent cuttings to propagate new plants.

EVERGREEN PLANTS

1. Protect with blinds and awnings from the hot low winter sun.
2. Cut back watering to absolute minimum to keep plants healthy.
3. Cut greenery if available for Christmas garlands.
4. Clean leaves prior to Christmas with a beer/milk mix.
5. Transplant rooted cuttings at end of winter.
6. Give plants an end-of-winter trim – perhaps start a topiary project.
7. Give plants end-of-winter feed.

HERBS

1. Remove dead annual herbs and clean pots.
2. Cover semi-hardy herbs with plant cosies or fleece in colder locations.
3. Take and plant up root cuttings of perennial herbs.
4. Ensure containers do not become waterlogged.
6. Give an end-of-winter tidy up.
7. Give an end-of-winter feed.

FRUIT GROWING

1. Winter pruning of deciduous fruit trees.
2. Clean up strawberry barrel or trough and plant runners in pots for new or replacement plants.
3. Cut grape vines back hard and spray with propolis against fungal attacks.
4. Harvest citrus fruits as they become ripe.

5. Place a large plastic bag or sheet supported by wire hoops over strawberries to stimulate early crops.

6. Obtain containers and plant citrus trees or a vine.

7. Dry slices of excess harvests of citrus crops.

VEGETABLE GROWING

1. Cut back watering. Just keep soil moist.

2. Start off spring/summer vegetables from seeds.

3. Thin out carrots and beetroots when just big enough to include whole in salads.

4. Buy a mini worm-composter and start to recycle kitchen waste to produce own compost and fertiliser.

5. Enjoy your home-grown crops of ecological, fresh-that-day vegetables for Christmas.

6. Obtain next years seed catalogues and immediately place orders for mini vegetable seeds – they can run out..

7. Clean up pots etc. where crops have finished and improve compost for spring sowings or plantlets.

OTHER

1. Make up a plant theatre to improve display of plants.

2. Complete trellis project ready for spring planting of climbers.

3. Construct a growing table for a plant collection or growing vegetables.

4. While tourists are not around browse ceramic shops for interesting containers, tiles and murals.

5. Tile lower walls Spanish-style.

Plant List, Vocabulary and Index

The Plant List gives English, Spanish and botanical names and page numbers for descriptions of each plant.

The Vocabulary includes the following sections:

1. Types of plants
2. Places for plants
3. Containers
4. Parts of plants
5. Measurements
6. Materials
7. Tools

The translations of the names of specific flowering/evergreen plants, fruits, herbs and vegetables have been provided separately in the relevant parts.

Part Four: Flowering/evergreen plants
Part Eight: Fruit trees and plants
Part Seven: Herbs
Part Nine: Vegetables
Part Ten: Insects and diseases

Plant List

*Where the previous name is the same we have entered 'ditto'

NAMES – **English,** Spanish, *Botanical* *	Page
Aechmea, ditto, *Aechmea*	87
Aeonium, Eonio, *Aeonium*	70
Agave attenuata, Agave atenuado, *Agave attenuata*	73
African lily, Agapantus, *Agapanthus*	84
Aloe - medicinal, Aloe vera, ditto	91
Angel's trumpet, Datura, *Datura brugmansia*	78
Asparagus fern, Protoasparagus densiflorus, ditto	82
Azalea, ditto, ditto	87
Barrel cactus, Echinocactus, *Echinocactus grusonii*	72
Bay, Laurel, *Laurus*	80
Begonia – painted leaf, Begonia rex, ditto	87
Belladona lily, Amarilis, *Amaryllis*	84
Bell flower, Campanula, ditto	75
Bergenia, ditto, *Bergenia Schmidt*	84
Bird of paradise bush, Poinciana, *Caesalpinia gilliepsii*	77
Bird of paradise, Ave de paraíso, *Strelitzia*	83
Bishop's cap, Astrofito, *Astrophytum myriosttigma*	72
Bottlebrush – weeping, Calistemon, ditto	77
Bougainvillea – dwarf, ditto - enano, *Bougainvillea mini Thai*	77
Bougainvillea – Glabra, ditto, ditto	86
Box, Boj, *Buxus sempervirens*	77
Bower vine, Pandorea jasminoides, ditto *(Bignonia)*	86
Busy lizzie, Alegría, *Impatiens*	89
Cabbage plant, Dracaena roja, *Cordyline australis*	74
Canary Island date palm, Palmera de Canarias – phoenix, *Phoenix canariensis*	74
Cape heather, Erica, *Erica e.gracilis*	78
Carnation-pink, Clavel, *Dianthus*	76
Cast-iron plant, Hoja de salón, *Aspidistra*	91
Cedar, Tuya, *Thuja*	83

English-Spanish Vocabulary

Note: This dictionary excludes the translation of the names of specific flowering plants, fruit trees, herbs and vegetables which are included in the relevant parts of the book.

1. TYPES OF PLANTS

Annual – un anual
Bamboo – un bambú
Bulb – un bulbo
Cactus – un cactus
Climber – una trepadora
Corm – un bulbo
Cultivar – una cultivada
Fruit tree – un frutal
Grass – la hierba
Ground cover – un progresivo
House plant – una planta de interior
Herbs – una hierba aromática
Palm – una palma
Perennial – un perenne
Rambler – una enredadera
Shrub – un arbusto
Shrub (climbing) – una trepadora
Succulent – un suculento
Tree – un árbol
Tree (evergreen) – un árbol de hoja perenne
Tree (deciduous) – un árbol de hoja caduca
Tree, dwarf – un árbol enano
Vegetable (green) – una verdura
Vegetable (general) – una hortaliza, una legumbre
Vegetable (pulses) – una leguminosa
Variety – una variedad
Vine, grape – una vid
Vine, other – una enredadera
Weed – una mala hierba

2. PLACES FOR PLANTS

Apartment – un apartamento, un piso
Apartment block – un edificio
Balustrade – una balaustrada
Balcony – un balcón
Ceiling – un techo
Container – un contenedor
Floor – un suelo
Penthouse – un ático
Railings – una baranda
Terrace – una terraza
Wall – un muro o una pared
Windowsill – un alféizar

3. CONTAINERS

Amphora – una ánfora
Bag – un saco
Barrel – un barril
Basket – un capacho
Bottle – una botella
Box – un cartón
Bowl – una escudilla o un tazón
Bucket – un cubo
Container – un contenedor
Grow bag – un bolso de cultivo
Growing table – una mesa de cultivo o una huerta urbana
Jug – un jarro
Plant pot – una maceta
Potato barrel – un barril de patatas
Raised bed – un macizo elevado
Seed box – una caja de simientes
Sprayer – un pulverizador
Strawberry barrel – un barril para fresones
Tub – una cubeta

Ten-tub vegetable garden – una huerta de diez cubetas
Tray, seed – una bandeja de semillero
Water butt – una tina para el agua
Watering can – una regadera
Window box – una jardinera de ventana

4. PARTS OF PLANTS

Bark – la corteza
Blossom – los flores
Branch – una rama
Bud – un brote
Bud (flower) – un capullo
Bud (leaf) – una yema
Cutting – un esqueje
Flower – una flor
Flower head – una cabezuela
Fruit – una fruta
Graft – un injerto
Ground cover – un progresivo
Leaf – una hoja
Perfume – un perfume
Plantlet – una plántula
Pollen – el polen
Root – una raíz
Seed – una semilla
Seed head – una cabezuela
Seedling – una plántula
Spray of flowers – una ramita
Stem – un tallo
String of onions – una ristra
Texture – la textura
Trunk – un tronco
Twig – una ramita

5. MEASUREMENTS

Centimetre – un centímetro
Metre – un metro
Kilo – un kilo
Litre – un litro

Cubic centimetre (cc) – centímetro cúbico
Basketful – un capacho lleno
Bucketful – un cubo lleno
Tea spoonful – una cucharita
Desert spoonful – una cucharada
Cup – una taza

6. APARTMENT GARDEN MATERIALS

Cane – una caña
Chippings – la gravilla suelta
Chippings, lava – la gravilla de lava
Compost – un abono vegetal
Compost, potting – un abono para macetas
Compost, seed – un abono para un semillero
Fertiliser – un abono
Fertiliser, foliar – un abono foliar
Fertiliser, granular – un abono granulado
Fertiliser, liquid – un abono liquido
Fertiliser, pearl – una perla fertilizante
Fertiliser, soluble – un abono soluble
Fleece – una malla térmica, el fleece
Fungicide – un fungicida
Garlic clove – un diente de ajo
Gloves – unos guantes
Grit – el cascajo
Herbicide – un herbicida
Insecticide – un insecticida
Labels, plastic – una etiqueta de plástico
Manure – estiércol
Mulch – mantillo
Moisture metre – un contador de humedad
Neem – el Neem
Netting – la red
Peat – la turba
Pesticide – un pesticida
Ph meter – un Ph metro
Plant – una planta
Pond, molded – un estanque moldeado

Post – un poste
Propolis – el propoleo
Rainwater – el agua de lluvia
Rock – una roca
Sack – un saco
Sand – la arena
Seeds – las semillas
Sheet plastic (solid) – una hoja de plástico
Sheet plastic (woven) – una malla de plástico
Soil – el suelo, la tierra
Stake – un rodrigón
String – la cuerda
Sulphur powder – el polvo de azufre
Thermometer – un termómetro
Timer – un interruptor horario
Tree – un árbol
Twine – el hilo

7. APARTMENT GARDEN NOUNS
Allotment – un huerto
Awning – un toldo
Bed, seed – un macizo
Bed, vegetable – un bancal
Bed, raised – un bancal elevado
Blind – un toldo
Garden– el jardin
Garden, vegetables – un huerto
Garden, fruit – una jardín frutero
Gardener – el jardinero
Climate, macro – un macroclima
Climate, micro – un microclima
Climate, nano – un nanoclima
Cloche – una campana
Companion plant – una planta beneficial
Composter – un compostador
Container – un container
Disease – una enfermedad
Diversity – una diversidad

Door – una puerta
Doorway – una entrada
Drainage – el drenaje
Drought – una sequía
Fence – una cerca
Flower bed – un cuadro, un macizo
Frost, air – una escarcha de aire
Frost, ground – una escarcha
Furniture – los muebles
Garden frame – un mini invernadero
Gardening, vegetables – horticultura
Greenhouse – un invernadero
Growing circle – un circlo de cultivo
Gutter – un canalón
Hail – el granizo
Hedge – un seto
Hole – un hoyo
Hose – una manguera
House – una casa
Injury – una herida
Insect – un insecto
Irrigation system – un sistema de irrigación
Lunar calendar – un calendario lunar
Mirror – un espejo
Mound, earth – un montón de tierra
Mulch – un alcolchado
Mural – un mural
Nature – la naturaleza
Orchard – un huerto de frutales
Painting – un cuadro
Path – una vereda/senda
Passageway – un pasillo
Patio – un patio
Pergola – una pérgola
Pest – una plaga
Plant – una planta
Plantlet – una plántula
Pollination – la polinación
Pond – un estanque
Property – una propiedad

Rain – la lluvia
Railings – las barandillas
Rockery – un jardín de rocalla
Row – una hilera
Seat – una silla
Seed bed – un semillero
Shade – la sombra
Shed garden – un cobertizo
Shrub – un arbusto
Shrubbery – los arbustos
Snow – la nieve
Sun – el sol
Sunshine – la luz del sol
Sun hat – un sombrero
Terrace – una terraza
Tie – una atadura
Tool – un útil
Trellis – un enrejado
Umbrella – un quitasol
Vegetable – una verdura
Vegetable plot – un huerto

View – una vista
Water – el agua
Water, rain – el aqua de lluvia
Water butt – una tina/un barril para el agua
Wall – un muro
Watering system – un sistema de riego
Weed – una mala hierba
Weather – el tiempo
Wildlife – la fauna
Windbreak – una abrigada
Window – una ventana
Windowsill – un alféizar
Wormery – un vermicompostador
Worm – una lombriz
Yard – un patio, un corral
Water – el agua
Weedkiller – un herbicida
Wire – el alambre
Wood – la madera
Worm, earth – una lombriz
Worm compost – el humus de lombriz

Index

Useful Addreses and Sources of Information

This is a list of suppliers that have products useful to keen apartment gardeners. They either deliver by mail order or will be found in garden centres, horticultural shops or agricultural cooperatives not only in Spain but also in other countries around the Med.

Ecological insecticides, fungicides and fertilisers – www.neudorff.com, www.seipasa.com, www.compo.es, www.floragard.com, www.trabe.net

Brand names of general ecological insecticide 'neem' – Neem, Nim, Ain, Manem

Ecological snail baits – www.neudorff.com, www.seipasa.com

Ecological soil improver – www.terracottem, www.terra-vida.com

Rain water collection tanks – www.graf-water. com, www.grafiberica.com

Water improver – www.viaqua.ie

Growing tables – invertem@invertem.com, www.sabatergrup.com

Trellis, gazeboes, planters etc. for penthouses – www.unopiu.it, www.unopiu.es

Raised beds, strawberry and potato barrels – www.harrodhorticulture.com, www.organiccaloque.com

Ergonomic pruners – www.fiscars.com

Dwarf (*enano*) fruit trees – www.soljardi.com

Seeds for tropical/sub-tropical/ Mediterranean plants– www.chilternseeds. co.uk, www.jungleseeds.co.uk, www.plant-world-seeds.co.uk,

www.kokopelli.assoc.fr, www.sanbi.org.za / seedroom@sanbi.org.za

Seeds for Spanish wild species – www.semillassilvestres.com

Plants of Mediterranean native species – www.cultidelta.com, olivier.filippi@wanadoo.fr

Rare bulbs – www.heritagebulbs.com (Ireland), www.blombulbs.com (UK), www.capeseedandbulbs.com (South Africa), seedroom@sanbi.org.za. (South Africa), www.bulbsargence.com (France).

Roses – www.davidaustinroses.com (Spain), www.cantsroses.co.uk (UK).

Vegetable seeds suitable for terraces – www.suttons-seeds.co.uk, www.thompson-morgan.com, www.chilternseeds.co.uk, www.organiccaloque.com, www.italianseedcompany.co.uk (All previous UK), www.germisem.com (Portugal), www.wildaboutveg.com (Ireland), www.semillasmadretierra.com (Spain), www.kokopelli.assoc.com (France), www.vilmorin.com (France),

Solar cookers for terraces – www.alsol.es

Mini worm-composters – www.wigglywigglers.co.uk

Sister books by authors Clodagh and Dick Handscombe published by Santana Books:

Your Garden in Spain – From planning to planting and maintenance
ISBN 978-84-89954-67-0 Published by Santana Books 2007

Growing Healthy Fruit in Spain – From strawberries to oranges and water melons
ISBN 978-84-89954-62-5 Published by Santana Books 2007

Growing Healthy Vegetables in Spain – From sprouting seeds to giant pumpkins
ISBN 978-84-89954-53-3 Published by Santana Books 2006